CONTENTS

PREFACE &
ACKNOWLEDGEMENTS

What we are all experiencing worldwide is not just another political event.

"This is not simply another four-year election. This is a crossroads in the history of our civilization that will determine whether or not we, the people, reclaim control over our government." - POTUS

He's not just talking about the U.S. Government, or any single nation's government. He means <u>Reclaim Control Over the Governing of the World from the Worldwide Criminal Mafia.</u>

This will transform the world for 1,000 years!
Literally.
Where do I get that?
From the Bible is all...
This is the Great Awakening.
We are fighting the New World Order in this epic Battle of Armageddon.

Good versus Evil.

We are embarking on 1,000 years of peace and health and wealth for all of humanity! The Bible calls this the Millennial Kingdom of Christ as in-
   "His Kingdom come, His will be done on earth as it is in Heaven."
The Kingdom of Christ is when:
  - Christ assumes His authority as King on earth,
  - Christ removes those who have usurped His throne,
  - The "Good Guys" finally rule the earth with Him,
    straightening out this whole mess the Deep State (DS)
    criminals have made!

No matter what the enemy tries, there's nothing he can do to stop this! We were told from the beginning,

1

Big.

Bigger!

BIGGEST!!!

This truly is the BIGGEST! That sounds Impossible! Outrageous! Too good to be true!

But the Bible is chock-full of this promise. Sadly most 'Bible scholars" don't recognize it yet. Just like so-called "scholars" have missed what the LORD was doing from time immemorial! Just like we have been under mass deception by "experts" for years!

You are welcome to simply believe what religious pundits, and political pundits, and media pundits, and every other pundit says, OR

You are invited to join the white hats in the fight to take back our world, and have your eyes opened to what the LORD has promised over and over in His Word, and how He is fulfilling those promises in our Day!

You will be very glad you found this book.

That leads me to a very important point. Thank you to my Freedom Force Battalion. You're the most wonderful patriot brothers and sisters!! I'm so glad we've joined in this Great Day on our YouTube site. I love that we share important information and gear up for battle, AND that we pray together, and for each other. In the midst of the fog of war, we keep each other going!

Thank you so much for joining me and receiving my videos with grace and faith, even when I say something you might not have considered. And thank you for compelling me to take on this book project, and for praying it through! I love you and appreciate you so much! We'll forever know that we were in this Great Battle together!

And, of course, thank you Mr. Wonderful for supporting me in a thousand ways, so I can follow the LORD's calling on my life. You are the most amazing husband a girl could ever ask for! You are my sounding board, my confidant, and the one who helps me breathe.

Thank you to all the patriots everywhere who do battle in their pajamas! Thank you to those who have used their mad skills to help us win this battle online, and who can decode posts that leave normies like me dazed and confused. Thank you to the white hats in the White House, and in Congress, and in the FBI, and DOJ, and CIA, and NSA, and every other ABC agency who risked their lives and everything they hold dear, to expose the criminal Deep State. Thank you to the proud and brave military men and women whose might made this victory possible. Hat tip to you all. And we extend our undying gratitude for the lives of our precious grandchildren and future progeny.

And Thank You President Trump for laying down the wonderful life you enjoyed, and for risking it all, not only for us in America, but for the entire world. We owe you a debt we can never repay. We love you.

Most importantly, thank You LORD Jesus for coming to rescue us. The enemy had us down, but You are faithful to Your Word, and You are setting us free from his every evil scheme. Tell the angels thank you for waking us up and gathering patriots together from all over the world!

All Your promises are Yea and Amen, and we will see the goodness of the LORD in the land of the living! We will see the day when nation will not rise against nation, and there will be no more war. We will see the day when the earth will be filled with the knowledge of the LORD, as the waters fill the sea. We will see the day when the young will proclaim the truth, the old will dream dreams of a long life, and youth will have visions of a bright future. We will see every lying mouth stopped, and all become accountable to You, King Jesus. We will see every knee bow and hear every tongue confess that You ALONE are LORD! We will look for our enemy, and won't be able to find them. And You will reign on earth forever and ever. Thank You LORD for Your unfailing love, and for shedding Your blood to free us from every plot of the enemy. Thank You that You continually pour out Your love on each of us. We love you back.

CHAPTER 1
REVOLUTION

Everyone has to admit they have never seen anything like what has been happening on earth since mid 2015. Come to think of it, it started right around the time Donald J. Trump announced he was running for President of the United States. Clearly something powerful is happening worldwide. But what? Why? Will things go back to the way they were before? Should I be worried?

That's what this book is about.

Some call it The Great Awakening. And it is VERY GOOD NEWS.

The strangest part is that even though millions have been awaiting this Day, very few even realize THIS IS IT! The Bible calls it the GREAT DAY of the LORD!

Now, don't be scared! Revelation is not what we have been told, with the world blowing up into a gigantic fireball. That was like the Wizard of Oz trying to scare us. Yes, we are at war with the worldwide mafia cabal, and they will try their evil tricks, but our Victory is sure! It will be a bumpy ride, but we will get through it. The LORD is with us. He is leading us. There is no need to fear. No need to panic. (At least not for us.)

I'm torn between making this very simplistic, OR deep-diving into each and every verse in the Book of the Revelation. I'm going to try to strike somewhere in the middle. So, if many of these verses and concepts are new to you, just hang in there with me. I'm going to break it down so it doesn't sound like a college course on Shakespeare! I just don't want to skip over passages that would cause more questions for those who are more familiar with this subject.

I have used several Bible passages from the King James Version, taking out the thees and thous, so it sounds more modern. If you don't catch everything the first time through, (or the second or third), that is AOK. Be patient. Ask the LORD for understanding. He promised to guide us into all truth.

> As Peter said, "some things hard to understand, which those who are unlearned and unstable twist..." (2nd Peter 3:16)

Does that mean we shouldn't search for the truth? Of course, not! As we study more, we have more light, which dispels the darkness and confusion. The Word is our only source of reliable light! So let's dive right in!

CHAPTER 2 EVERYONE'S WAITING ON A MESSIAH

You probably know that Christians worldwide have been anticipating the imminent return of Christ. Most Biblical scholars believe this, based on the prophecies in books like Daniel, and from the very words of Christ Himself. And what's really a "coincidence," is that:

- those who follow Judaism are awaiting their Meschiach, and

- Christians are waiting on our Messiah,

- true Muslims are awaiting their Mahdi,

- Hindus are awaiting their Krishna, and

- Buddhists are waiting on Maitreya.

And they all expect Him to bring peace on earth between all people. What a **"coincidence!"** But maybe it's not a coincidence. Maybe Christ will guide each one of these groups into the truth, removing the deception, and that's how we will **all** come under His authority as King of kings! Similar to this verse in Ephesians 2:15:

> *"Having abolished in his flesh the enmity, even the law of commandments contained in ordinances; **for to make in himself of two peoples one new man, so making peace;**"*

Christ will bring all His people of the world together in peace, breaking down the deception that has divided us.

And while we are at it, let's make sure we are all on the same page when we read a verse about Israelites or Jews or Hebrews. When you read the word Israelite or Jew or Hebrew, sometimes the context is about the physical lineage, but most times it is talking about "God's family." The word Israel includes believers from the physical lineage of the "lost tribes" of Israel that have been scattered worldwide. (See "Missing Links Discovered in Assyrian Tablets" by E. Raymond Capt for where the lost tribes are now.) And the names Israel and Jew many times include believers by "adoption" too!

Historically, Israelites are the ten northern tribes, the Jews are the two southern tribes, and Hebrews are Abraham's seed. Depending on the context, the name Jew could mean:

- a person with the physical lineage of Judah, or

- fake Jews (some are actually Edomites from Esau), or

- Messianic Jews (Judahite believers in Christ), or

- simply Jews in a general sense, encompassing all of God's people.

You see the subject is complex! Believers from every nation are what the Bible calls **True Israelites** and **True Jews**. This is very important. The enemy has used this subject to cause unbelievable confusion. Yes, there are differences because of ethnicity. But the most important distinction, especially for this book, is to see God's promises to His entire family, whether by blood lineage or by "adoption."

"Those who are of faith, are sons of Abraham." (Galatians 3:7)

"For he is not a Jew, which is one outwardly; neither is that circumcision, which is outward in the flesh: But he is a Jew, which is one inwardly; and circumcision is that of the heart, in the spirit, and not in the letter; whose praise is not of men, but of God." (Romans 2:28-29)

"There is neither Jew nor Greek, there is neither bond nor free, there is neither male nor female: for you are all one in Christ Jesus. And if you be Christ's, then are you Abraham's seed, and heirs according to the promise." (Galatians 3:28-29)

In case you'd like to know why Christians worldwide are anticipating Christ's return, here are some conversations our LORD Jesus had with His disciples:

*"And if I go and prepare a place for you, **I will come again**, and receive you to myself; that where I am, there you may be also."* (John 14:3)

*"When the **Son of Man shall come in his glory, and all the holy angels with him, then shall he sit upon the throne of his glory**. And before him shall be gathered all nations: and he shall separate them one from another, as a shepherd divides his sheep from the goats. And he shall set the sheep on his right hand, but the goats on the left."* (Matthew 25:31-33)

*"And as he sat upon the mount of Olives, the disciples came unto him privately, saying, Tell us, when shall these things be? and what shall be **the sign of your coming**, and of the end of the age?"* (Matthew 24:3)

*"Looking for that blessed hope, and **the glorious appearing of the great God and our Savior Jesus Christ.**"* (Titus 2:13)

In case you'd like to know why many believe Christ's return is imminent, check this out. This prophecy goes back 2,600 years ago, where the LORD gave King Nebuchadnezzar a dream of a great statue, depicting all the future world empires. It has happened just as the dream foretold.

In 612 BC the prophet Daniel interpreted King Nebuchadnezzar's dream of future world empires - the Babylonian Empire, the

Medo-Persian Empire, the Greek Empire, the Roman Empire, and then the Divided Kingdom.

Each of the empires has come and gone, except for the last one. Do you see where we are on the timeline? We are down to the 10 TOES!!

We have been in the Divided Kingdom since the fall of the Roman Empire. The Divided Kingdom is the last empire before the Kingdom of Christ. This is based on King Nebuchadnezzar's disturbing dream, which Daniel interpreted (recorded in Daniel 2) below:

Daniel's Interpretation

Babylonian Kingdom

> 36 "This was the dream; now we will tell its interpretation before the king. 37 You, O king, are the king of kings, to whom the God of heaven has given the kingdom, the power, the strength and the glory; 38 and wherever the sons of men dwell, or the beasts of the field, or the birds of the sky, He has given them into your hand and has caused you to rule over them all. You are the head of gold."

Medo-Persian Empire and Greek Empire

> 39 "After you there will arise another kingdom inferior to you, then another third kingdom of bronze, which will rule over all the earth."

Roman Empire

40 "Then there will be a fourth kingdom as strong as iron; inasmuch as iron crushes and shatters all things, so, like iron that breaks in pieces, it will crush and break all these in pieces."

Divided Kingdom

41 "In that you saw the feet and toes, partly of potter's clay and partly of iron, it will be a divided kingdom; but it will have in it the toughness of iron, inasmuch as you saw the iron mixed with common clay. 42 As the toes of the feet were partly of iron and partly of pottery, so some of the kingdom will be strong and part of it will be brittle. 43 And in that you saw the iron mixed with common clay, they will combine with one another in the seed of men; but they will not adhere to one another, even as iron does not combine with pottery."

The Divine Kingdom

44 "In the days of those kings the God of heaven will set up a kingdom which will never be destroyed, and that kingdom will not be left for another people; it will crush and put an end to all these kingdoms, but it will itself endure forever. 45 Inasmuch as you saw that a stone was cut out of the mountain without hands and that it crushed the iron, the bronze, the clay, the silver and the gold, the great God has made known to the king what will take place in the future; so the dream is true and its interpretation is trustworthy." (Daniel 2)

So, the point is, there are no other empires that are to come, before the Kingdom of Christ. And the Kingdom of Christ will crush all the other kingdoms, but it will endure forever! YaHOOOOO!

Almost all modern scholars have agreed that we have been living in the Divided Kingdom. So what is this Divided Kingdom like? First of all, this empire has many nations but they have been ruled by a vicious powerful tyrant beast. Where do I get that? Good ole Daniel again. This time Daniel 7.

Daniel said, "I was looking in my vision by night, and behold, the four winds of heaven were stirring up the great sea. 3 And four great beasts were coming up from the sea, different from

*one another. 4 The first was like a lion and had the wings of an eagle. I kept looking until its wings were plucked, and it was lifted up from the ground and made to stand on two feet like a man; a human mind also was given to it. 5 And behold, another beast, a second one, resembling a bear. And it was raised up on one side, and three ribs were in its mouth between its teeth; and thus they said to it, 'Arise, devour much meat!' 6 After this I kept looking, and behold, another one, like a leopard, which had on its back four wings of a bird; the beast also had four heads, and dominion was given to it. 7 **After this I kept looking in the night visions, and behold, a fourth beast, dreadful and terrifying and extremely strong; and it had large iron teeth. It devoured and crushed and trampled down the remainder with its feet; and it was different from all the beasts that were before it, and it had ten horns.** 8 While I was contemplating the horns, behold, another horn, a little one, came up among them, and three of the first horns were pulled out by the roots before it; and behold, **this horn possessed eyes like the eyes of a man and a mouth uttering great boasts.**"*

Notice the **10** Toes of Daniel 2? And the **10** Horns of Daniel 7?

Those represent the DIVIDED KINGDOM.

The LAST Kingdom before the Kingdom of Christ!

We have been under the rule of this Divided Kingdom, which has been Devouring, and Crushing, and Trampling people down, all over the world. One look at North Korea's concentration camps, or China's slave labor, or Venezuela's starvation, or the Cultural and Health devastation in America, or the utter poverty in Africa, and on and on, and there is no doubt the Beast Daniel is referring to is the same as the Divided Kingdom.

Who would like to know what the animals represent? Meeeee! It is possible there are multiple interpretations that could apply... one interpretation with ancient empires... one interpretation with modern empires... both ruthless... both being valid. I'll tell you my thoughts on an interpretation with modern empires.

I see the lion with eagle's wings as the evil bloodline rulers of England. When we think of a nation symbolized by a lion, we think of England. And I think the two wings that were plucked off represent America! I love that interpretation because the eagle's wings stand on their feet and are given the mind of a man. That reminds me of what true Americans have always thought we were doing... having the heart of God's love for humanity. We just didn't know the traitors were using our money and military to harm humanity. But, America, under the leadership of President Trump, is finally fulfilling that role of saving humanity!

How about the bear? I'd say Russia. We think of Russia as the Great Bear. They have also been terribly used and abused by the New World Order (NWO), namely the Czars, Stalin, etc. But they have kicked out the globalist banksters! So Russia is awakening too!

How about the leopard with four wings and four heads and dominion? That one reminds me of Germany, with how they have been used by the NWO Nazis to dominate the world. The Third Reich supposedly fell after WWII, but we know the New World Order Nazis simply infiltrated every nation, morphing into the Fourth Reich, matching the four wings and four heads. Yep... the leopard sounds like the Nazi New World Order.

What about the Little Horn? Horns represent power. But this power is different from the power of the other horns.   This power seems smaller than the others, but utters great boasts, as if it somehow has more power than they do.

"possessed eyes like the eyes of a man and a mouth uttering great boasts." (verse 8)

What authority on earth is small, but pushes everybody around? Telling them what to do, against their will, as if they are god on earth? Any ideas? I believe the Little Horn is the United Nations. The UN is small, but boasts great power. It is obviously controlled by the New World Order.

13 *"I kept looking until the beast was slain, and its body was destroyed and given to the burning fire. I kept looking in the night visions, and behold, **with the clouds of heaven, One like a Son of Man was coming**,* *and He came up to the Ancient of Days and was presented before Him."* 14 *"And to Him was given dominion, glory and a kingdom, that all the peoples, nations and men of every language might serve Him. His dominion is an everlasting dominion which will not pass away; And His kingdom is one which will not be destroyed."* (Daniel 7:13-14)

Hallelujah!!!

The Beast was slain!

And its body was destroyed!

And the Son of Man was revealed in great power - symbolized by "the clouds of heaven." He was given dominion and the kingdom! Hallelujah again!

We see the same beautiful imagery in Daniel 2, where "The stone destroys the other empires and becomes a Huge Mountain!"

Of course, that Stone is Christ!

"And in the days of these kings shall the God of heaven set up a kingdom, which shall never be destroyed: and the kingdom shall not be left to other people, but it shall

break in pieces and consume all these kingdoms, and it shall stand for ever.

45 Forasmuch as you saw that the stone was cut out of the mountain without hands, and that it broke in pieces the iron, the brass, the clay, the silver, and the gold; the great God has made known to the king what shall come to pass hereafter." (Daniel 2)

Both Daniel 2 and Daniel 7 are pictures of Christ's Kingdom being established on earth! Each of the former evil empires is broken, along with their power to deceive humanity! Every kind of evil authority, whether it is rudimentary like clay, or powerful like iron, or loud and showy like brass, or even extraordinarily wealthy like silver and gold, will all be ground to powder! Thank You LORD, that You let us live on earth to see this Day! Thank You LORD that You are faithful to Your promises! Thank You LORD that Your Righteous Kingdom will be FOREVER! HALLELUJAH!!!

"And there was given him dominion, and glory, and a kingdom, that all people, nations, and languages, should serve him: his dominion is an everlasting dominion, which shall not pass away, and his kingdom that which shall not be destroyed." (Daniel 7:14)

We are the generation that is seeing His Kingdom come and His will being done on earth, as it is in Heaven!

Let that sink in......................... Hallelujah!

....

Before we go on, can we identify this terrible, Devouring, Crushing, Trampling Beast... the Divided Kingdom with 10 toes – 10 horns of crushing, dominating power? Those of you who are awake already know.

This is the New World Order. The Bloodlines. The Globalists. International Bankers who have controlled the Central Banks and puppet leaders in almost every nation.

NEW WORLD ORDER - The Triangle of Evil

1. Rothschilds/Payseurs - Head of Financial Control

2. Soros - Head of Political Control

3. House of Saud - Head of Human and Drug Trafficking

They have run a worldwide secret society web of minions as puppet leaders in governments, powerful players in Media, Hollywood, Religious Institutions, Education, Medical/Pharmaceuticals, Corrupt Judges, and Military, and Justice officials.

Some call them Illuminati... because they follow Lucifer, the "Angel of Light" who promises them "hidden knowledge," but they end up being filled with darkness and evil.

BLOODLINES

Astors	Onassis
Bundys	Reynolds
Collins	Rockefellers
DuPont	Rothschilds
Freeman	Russell
Kennedy	Van Duyn
Li	

They call themselves the "Elite"... but we know they are anything but.

They are ultra-wealthy international bankers/bloodline families (see the Fritz Springmeier's book on the Illuminati.) Rich. Powerful. Evil.

The Bible calls them the Anti-Christ... because EVERYTHING they do is OPPOSITE of Christ. Anti-Nation, Anti-Freedom, Anti-Health, Anti-Family, Anti-Faith, Anti-Law, Anti Anti Anti.

That is a LOT to take in, but it is absolutely critical that we understand who our enemy is so we can fight back, expose them, and break free from their tyranny. Make no mistake about it. Their power structure will crumble.

So... we see prophecies from ancient texts that have foretold a time when the evil kingdoms of earth will be destroyed, and there will finally be peace on earth. Every major religion is waiting for the imminent appearing of the Messiah. But, to be frank, if the Messiah were here, and we were dead asleep under mass deception, we wouldn't even recognize Him, or know who to fight in the Battle of Armageddon.

That's why we needed a GREAT AWAKENING! And that's what the next chapter is about!

CHAPTER 3
AWAKENING
HUMANITY

I heard of the GREAT AWAKENING all my life. But I never imagined what it would look like. I guess because zombies don't realize they are asleep. The prophet Ezekiel gave us an incredible picture of the Great Awakening... and most of us still didn't get it. Check out this wild picture of Ezekiel's vision!

Ezekiel wrote,

"The hand of the Lord was upon me, and carried me out in the spirit of the Lord, and set me down in the midst of the valley which was full of bones, And caused me to pass by them round about: and, behold, there were very many in the open valley; and, lo, they were very dry. And he said unto me, Son of man, can these bones live? And I answered, O Lord God, you know.

Again he said to me, Prophesy upon these bones, and say unto them, O dry bones, hear the word of the Lord. Thus says the Lord God unto these bones; Behold, I will cause breath to enter into you, and you shall live: And I will lay sinews upon you, and will bring up flesh upon you, and cover you with skin, and put breath in you, and you shall live; and ye shall know that I am the Lord.

So I prophesied as I was commanded: and as I prophesied, there was a noise, and behold a shaking, and the bones came together, bone to his bone. And when I beheld, lo, the sinews and the flesh came up upon them, and the skin covered them above: but there was no breath in them. Then said he unto me, Prophesy unto the wind, prophesy, son of man, and say to the wind, Thus said the Lord God; Come from the four winds, O breath, and breathe upon these slain, that they may live.

So I prophesied as he commanded me, and the breath came into them, and they lived, and stood up upon their feet, an exceeding great army." (Ezekiel 37: 1-10)

First of all... ew. A valley full of dead dry bones. Gross. Sorry to tell you, but that is humanity. We were massacred, and we didn't even know it. The swamp creatures are everywhere doing thousands of terrible things to destroy us. The LORD asked Ezekiel if these could live again. And Ezekiel rightly answered, "Only YOU know, LORD." In other words, "Lord only knows."

Then the LORD told Ezekiel to speak to the dead dry bones. Do you hear how crazy that sounds? LOL! Amazingly, Ezekiel did it! And even more amazingly, the bones responded!! "The foot bone connected to the ankle bone, and the ankle bone connected to the leg bone, the leg bone..." You get the point. "They heard the Word of the LORD!" (Are you singing the song with me?)

That is humanity, waking up! Hearing the Word of the LORD! Not from preachers, eh em false preachers. We have heard the Word of the LORD directly from Him! We heard Him tell us about the New World Order. And the pedophiles. And the human traffickers. And the money-making wars and diseases. And the chemtrails (geoengineering). And the puppet leaders. And the fake news from every direction! And... on and on and on. And we have heard Him tell us to expose the evil and take His kingdom by force!

"And from the days of John the Baptist until now the kingdom

of heaven suffers violence, and the violent (Patriots) *take it by force."* (Matthew 11:12)

That's what we're doing! Taking the Kingdom BY FORCE!

But to know the truth wasn't enough. We needed a push. We needed POWER. Bones connected together can't fight this demonic spiritual enemy. We could not have produced this movement... this GREAT AWAKENING of digital soldiers. Not with all the tweets and the videos and the screaming and crying we could muster.

So the LORD told Ezekiel to ask the Spirit to breathe on these slain. And Ezekiel again obeyed. And look at that! The bones were covered with muscles and skin and then they rose up... a MIGHTY ARMY!!!

That's us!

The Patriots!!!

The LORD is not only waking us up to what is going on, He is giving us power to fight!

We are living in the Great Day of the Great Awakening!!!

Every day, angels are waking more people up, and we all are coming out of our slumber. Realizing who our real enemy is! And we are joining the fight!

> *"And He will send His angels with a great sound of a **trumpet**, and **they will gather together His elect** from the four winds, from one end of heaven to the other."* (Matthew 24:31)

We are wiping the sleepy out of our eyes, and turning away from the darkness we were force-fed. We are coming out of the deception, little by little. We are in hot pursuit of truth, and sharing it like the Locust Army in Joel Chapter 2, going over the walls and through the windows, never breaking rank.

Joel Chapter 2 talks about gloom for the Deep State criminals... but victory for the LORD'S Army!

"*Blow the trumpet in Zion,*

(Trump is our Commander in Chief)

and sound an alarm in my holy mountain:

(Time for War against the Tyrants)

let all the inhabitants of the land tremble:

for the day of the LORD comes, for it is near at hand;

2 A day of darkness and of gloominess,

(for the New World Order)

a day of clouds and of thick darkness,

as the morning spread upon the mountains:

a great people and a strong;

there has not been ever the like,

neither shall be any more after it,

(the Greatest Ever Worldwide Patriots!)

even to the years of many generations.

(what we're experiencing is HISTORIC!)

3 A fire devours before them; and behind them a flame

burns: the land is as the garden of Eden before them,

and behind them a desolate wilderness; yea,

(Patriots destroying the Deep State!)

and nothing shall escape them. **(Anons are on it!)**

4 The appearance of them is as the appearance of horses; and as horsemen, so shall they run.

5 Like the noise of chariots on the tops of mountains shall they leap, like the noise of a flame of fire that devours the stubble, as a strong people set in battle array.

6 Before their face the people shall be much pained:

all faces shall be in dread.

(Deep State panic!)

7 They shall run like mighty men;

(We are in hot pursuit!)

they shall climb the wall like men of war;

and they shall march every one on his ways,

and they shall not break their ranks:

(Patriots stay together)

8 Neither shall one thrust another;

they shall walk every one in his path:

and when they fall upon the sword, they shall not be wounded.

9 They shall run to and fro in the city;

they shall run upon the wall,

they shall climb up into the houses;

(Patriots expose every lie)

they shall enter in at the windows like a thief.

(Patriot posts are EVERYWHERE!)

10 The earth shall quake before them; the heavens shall tremble:

(The world is in an uproar because the powerful are falling!)

the sun and the moon shall be dark,

(the brightest and mightiest are now despised)

and the stars shall withdraw their shining:

(the rich and famous "stars" are being exposed; chemtrails make the sky murky grey)

11 And the LORD shall utter his voice before his army:

for his camp is very great:

for he is strong that executes his word:

for the Day of the LORD is great and very terrible;

and who can abide it?

(Not one of the criminals will escape judgment)

We are patriots and have joined together which is all about God's

Plan that He has for us... to give us hope and a future.

He doesn't just want us to expose the lies. He wants us to take authority on earth. To rule in every position around the world, and take the kingdom by force! Imagine every judge, every police chief, every teacher and school administrator, every government leader, every business owner, and every media person, etc., working for God's glory, under the authority of Christ! WOW!

> *"You have made them into a kingdom, priests to serve our God, and they will reign on the earth."* (Revelation 5:10)

Did you catch that? **On Earth... reigning with Him.**

> *"And from the days of John the Baptist until now the kingdom of heaven suffers violence, and the violent take it by force." (Matthew 11:12)*

We have suffered enough violence! We are kicking in the NWO doors and taking our Country back! And our world back!

That is one of the reasons we named our YouTube channel "Freedom Force Battalion," because we have joined there to pray, and fight, and take the Kingdom of Christ by FORCE!

We have a playlist called "Bible Before Our Eyes" that decodes how Biblical battle scenes are being played out today!

We are David, killing the NWO Criminal Goliath!

We are Joshua, blowing the TRUMPets to bring down the walls of the Canaanites (cannibals).

We are Gideon, blowing the TRUMPets to defeat thousands of enemies with only 300 warriors!

We are Esther, thwarting Haman's evil plot to annihilate God's people! Just like them, we will defend ourselves and defeat all our enemies!

We are Deborah and Jael driving a stake through the skull of "Skull & Bones."

We are even seeing stories decoded, like when our LORD was the Good Samaritan telling the innkeeper He would return in two days... 2,000 years in God's time!

We are in an INFORMATION War... not primarily a war with tanks and guns. The most important thing to know is how we have been lied to! And how we expose the lies so everyone can come into the truth and be set free!! That's next...

CHAPTER 4
DECEPTION OF
THE MASSES

Now stick with me. Parts of this journey might be a little bumpy, because some of what we have been lead to believe has been merely deception to keep us in the dark. Deceivers have crept into every institution and we were unaware, even though we were warned in God's Word.

"For certain men crept in unawares, who were before of old ordained to this condemnation, ungodly men..." (Jude 1:4)

Some teachers have deceived others on purpose. Other teachers are deceiving, but they believe they are telling us the truth. I'm not writing this book to try to point out which are the Deceivers and which are the Deceived. The purpose of this book is to free us from the Deception!

I am not going into each and every error, but I will mention a few... because they are popular arguments I hear when we discuss that this is the Great Day of the LORD and we are currently fighting Armageddon against the Beast/New World Order.

We in the Great Awakening movement have been shocked to discover that political figures we have known and respected all our lives, have actually tricked us. Many are part of a worldwide mafia with a giant Get Rich Scheme through wars and disease and drugs, and worse. That is the topic of many other books.

The deception I want to draw your attention to is that **Deceivers** infiltrated the seminaries and churches and Christian entertainment, to trick us into standing down.

Did you get that?

Deceivers infiltrated the seminaries and churches and Christian entertainment, to trick us into STANDING DOWN.

So we would not IDENTIFY and FIGHT them.

What could they get us to believe that would cause us to STAND DOWN AND NOT FIGHT FOR OURSELVES AND OUR FAMILIES?

Ready for ERROR # 1 to be Exposed?

I really don't want to tell you because some of you will slam this book down, and throw it away.

But don't.

It's ESCAPE.

Huh?

They told us we would escape earth, and then the whole earth would be destroyed. So most believed it, and are expecting to escape and not have to fight the Beast. But that isn't true.

ERROR # 1 EXPOSED -
Christians escape earth in the Rapture and don't fight Armageddon. NO!

It's Classic Brainwashing.

Take a truth. Twist the truth into a lie. Repeat it often, from every source, especially from trusted sources, like pastors, and people usually accept it. Classic. This particular lie is called Rapture. And it worked like a charm, literally. Most Christians are not even trying to identify the Beast of Daniel and Revelation, because they have been misled to think the Beast will appear AFTER Christians escape in the Rapture. So they won't have to fight the Beast anyway. Good one, New World Order.

The verse they twist into deception, 1st Thessalonians 4:16-17, is not about escaping earth. It is about the Great Day of Consummation when we will receive our incorruptible bodies! We are not escaping earth. The LORD is going to reign on earth for 1,000 years, and we will reign with Him here, not on a cloud somewhere! The clouds symbolize power and authority, not escape.

Here's the passage I'm talking about:

> "For the Lord himself shall descend from heaven with a shout, with the voice of the archangel, and with the trump of God: and the dead in Christ shall rise first: Then we which are alive and remain shall be caught up together with them in the clouds, to meet the Lord in the air: and so shall we ever be with the Lord." (1st Thessalonians 4:16-17)

This verse is not about escaping earth and flying in the air. I know it is difficult to wrap our heads around the truth, especially if we've believed these verses the way we were taught. That's why they call it DECEPTION. We will come out of all the deception, eventually. So let's get started! Let's shake off all the lies!

Ready for more lies to be exposed? Really?

ERROR # 2 EXPOSED -
Pre-Trib, Mid-Trib, Post-Trib Rapture. NO!

This whole discussion is DIVERSION. I'm not going to play. The point is NOT about trying to figure out when the Rapture takes place. Because Rapture is a DIVERSION too! There is NOT a seven-year worldwide cataclysmic tribulation either. The whole discussion is one gigantic deception diversion. Most who "study" the Revelation get so focused on whether the Rapture is Pre-Tribulation, Mid-Tribulation, or Post-Tribulation that they don't actually study the Revelation! A DIVERSION inside a DIVERSION! Another good one, New World Order!

That's all I'm going to say about that.

ERROR # 3 EXPOSED -
One Left, One Taken verse is about Rapture.   NO!

These two passages below SEEMINGLY contradict each other, logistically. But the riddle has been solved! The NWO infiltrated and told us the "One Taken" is the "Rapture." That was mass deception.

> *"And He will send His angels with a great sound of a trumpet, and they will gather together His elect from the four winds, from one end of heaven to the other."* (Matthew 24:31)

Versus

> *"For the coming of the Son of Man will be just like the days of Noah. For as in those days before the flood they were eating and drinking, marrying and giving in marriage, until the day that Noah entered the ark, and they did not understand until the flood came and took them all away; so will the coming of the Son of Man be.*
>
> *"Then there will be two men in the field; one will be taken and one will be left.*
>
> *"Two women will be grinding at the mill; one will be taken and one will be left.* (Matthew 24:37-41)

So, the questions are: Who is Taken? Who is Left? Who is Gathered? Good guys? Bad guys?

RIDDLE SOLVED!

Who is Gathered?   The angels *gathered* the warriors from all over the world, to fight the enemy New World Order.

The Armageddon battle is an INFORMATION WAR. Our battlefield is the Internet. The angels do not have to MOVE us to a physical battlefield. Angels have gathered us from all over the world and we are fighting from our laptops! (Of course, we certainly have military who will physically accomplish whatever is needed.)

When you think of "field," don't think about an area of land. Think about a "profession."

Who is "taken" from the "field?"   All the criminals will be removed from their positions of authority and they will no longer be able to hurt the people, through "fields" of bad medicine, media, surveillance, GMOs, technology, etc.

Who is "left" in the "field?"   Those who will use the "fields" of study for good, instead of evil, will be left to run the companies and organizations, media and education, etc.   Which means health, wealth, and peace will permeate the entire world!

ERROR # 4 EXPOSED -
The Battle of Armageddon is against the entire world of unbelievers! NO!

They have lead us to believe that when the LORD appears, there will be worldwide nuclear devastation and calamity. That Armageddon fear-mongering propaganda is NOT TRUE! The truth is that Christ and His army of faithful patriots are fighting the Beast, and peace will settle over the earth because those who have been causing such turmoil and suffering and deception WILL BE STOPPED!

Did you catch that?! Armageddon is Good versus Evil. Patriots against the Beast – the New World Order – these creeps who worship Lucifer and get their power and wealth from doing evil. They are the ones who took the "Mark of Evil" (the Mark of the Beast)! They have done unspeakable crimes against humanity, and they will pay dearly.   The LORD is saving us from their tyrannical, destructive rule! I repeat. The Battle of Armageddon is the Battle of Good vs Evil... not a worldwide annihilation of all of humanity! Now THAT'S Great News!

Everything we are doing to expose the corruption and lies is helping us win this battle of Armageddon! People are waking up and rising up to destroy the tyrants and their evil from the face of the earth.

ERROR # 5 EXPOSED -
Armageddon is a Physical War in the Jezreel Valley between a "Nation from the North" and Iraq. NO!

All of the Bible has come alive since the Great Awakening began, especially since realizing the New World Order is the Beast of Revelation. So I'm really not intending to be disrespectful to people who explain these passages without this information/ revelation. But I am trying to shed light on these passages in view of what we have learned recently.

No doubt, the deceivers have tried to send us on a wild goose chase. And those who are deceived, unwittingly pass on the deception.... and so on and on and on.

First off, we know that Armageddon is NOT a physical battle. We are fighting a spiritual war of Good versus Evil. We are fighting a "Worldwide Mafia Cabal of satanists." Armageddon is NOT a war between nations, as we typically think of nations. So when we read prophecies from books like Jeremiah and Isaiah, loaded with symbolism, we have to take this into account. Babylon is the New World Order. The Army from the North is the worldwide Patriots, which is the same army of Revelation 14 and Joel 2. When you read Jeremiah 50 about the "Nation from the North" in this light, you know it's talking about the Patriots destroying Babylon/NWO.

> *"For out of the north there comes up a nation against her, which shall make her land desolate, and none shall dwell therein: they shall remove, they shall depart, both man and beast."* (Jeremiah 50:3)

> *"I will raise and cause to come up against Babylon an assembly of great nations from the north country: and they shall set themselves in array against her; from there she shall be taken: their arrows shall be as of a mighty expert man; none shall return in vain."* (Jeremiah 50:9)

Just read the destruction we are wreaking on the New World Order, and you know this passage is talking about the Patriots.

> *14 "Put yourselves in array against Babylon round about: all you that bend the bow, shoot at her, spare no arrows: for she has sinned against the Lord.*

15 Shout against her round about: she has given her hand: her foundations are fallen, her walls are thrown down: for it is the vengeance of the Lord: take vengeance upon her; as she has done, do unto her." (Jeremiah 50)

That's **us** shooting Truth Arrows! Sparing none! And **we** are "doing unto her as she has done"! Notice it says, "her foundations are fallen," as in "Babylon (NWO) is Fallen!"

ERROR # 6 EXPOSED -
The Mark of the Beast is a Physical Mark/Chip required on all of humanity! NO!

This deception caused many to believe that God was going to destroy every man, woman, and child who took a Mark of the Beast tattoo or a chip in order to survive and save their families. Can you imagine? The LORD would never punish people for that! The Mark of the Beast has nothing to do with tattoos or chips at all! That is NOT the Mark of the Beast.

The Mark of the Beast is the Mark of PURE EVIL - it is satanic rituals and utter lawlessness. This is the "mark" that the New World Order minions have taken in order to gain wealth and privilege. They have been willing to do anything and say anything so they could be part of this "elite" club. These people are SICK!

> *"And the second beast required all people small and great, rich and poor, free and slave, to receive a mark on their right hand or on their forehead, so that **no one could buy or sell unless he had the mark**— the name of the beast or the number of its name."* (Revelation 13)

Here is the explanation of this mis-taught passage: In order to benefit financially, and receive positions and power, **all kinds of people, from all over the world,** have joined this evil secret society. It doesn't say every man, woman, and child, but all KINDS of people. Think about it. Have most people been **truly free** to buy and sell? To gain true wealth? **NO!** The stock market is rigged. The education system is rigged. The jobs are rigged.

The prices make it almost impossible to survive without going into debt slavery!

Only the minions of the New World Order cabal have truly had the power to buy and sell, and become rich and powerful, while the rest of us have been left outside, to struggle and lose our health and wealth.

Angry yet?

We have had tribulation on a mass worldwide scale... from Venezuela to North Korea to China to Africa to the financial and health and cultural devastation in America and all around the world. The world almost collapsed into complete slavery, but thank the LORD we are in the GREAT AWAKENING. The whole world is waking up! And casting out these evil tyrants!

If you have learned of the evils of human trafficking that have been done by the New World Order, and how people have joined in league with them to enslave humanity, they perfectly fit the description of the Beast of Revelation. These people are literally demon-possessed and have taken on the Mark of the Beast by committing unspeakable rituals. They have rigged everything so they are the only ones who have been able to gain true wealth, while we became poorer and enslaved. That is what the Mark of the Beast is... not the ridiculous and disrespectful notion that the LORD will destroy people who take a chip to save their families. The truth is that those who have done horrifying satanic rituals WILL be destroyed! This is the truth. We are all coming out of the deception that has been force-fed to the masses. Finally!

Those of us who studied the Revelation, were force-fed the popular explanations, which left us scratching our heads because none of them made sense, or jibed with Scripture. But now we realize it was filled with deception to hide the Beast/ New World Order!

ERROR # 7 EXPOSED -
The third temple MUST be built before the Battle of

Armageddon. NO!

And they also say that the "Anti-Christ must go and sit in that temple and proclaim himself as god." Well, my response is, "the Beast would never allow that to happen!" Because that would awaken the masses! So long as the temple is never built, there can be no Anti-Christ to go sit inside it! And that prevents Christians from ever identifying the Beast of Revelation, and the New World Order Beast can continue destroying the world all day long! Good one, New World Order.

Get it? Imagine you're a thief. You tell people that they will know the bank has been robbed when the front door is broken into. But you rob the bank, going through the back door! The people never catch on! And you laugh, and Laugh, and LAUGH!

"Sitting in the temple and proclaiming himself to be god" is symbolism. It means that the Anti-Christ/New World Order/Beast acts like they are god on earth. Telling everyone what to do. Demanding absolute obedience. Financially enslaving. Removing prayer. Forcing Anti-God education down our throats. Flooding the airwaves with lies and filth against God. No doubt this describes the NWO perfectly!

Catching on to their little game?

The Beast/New World Order works perfectly, so long as the masses never put two and two together! Once we do, their little evil scheme comes unglued! And THAT, my friends, is what has happened! The entire WORLD has awakened to our true enemy... the New World Order Bloodline Luciferian Globalist International Bankers. Everyone except the Church at large. Shockingly, most Christians are still sitting on their hands, waiting for the third temple. If believers are waiting for their church leaders to identify the Beast, and Armageddon, and the Great Awakening, they are likely in for a long wait.

Eyeroll.

ERROR # 8 EXPOSED -

The Tribulation hasn't happened yet.   NO!

I shake my head whenever I hear someone say "The Tribulation" hasn't happened yet. Really? Are you kidding me? The world is in ruins! As President Trump says, this is our last chance to save our Country. And even the world.

China is a Communist Slave State.

Venezuelans are literally starving under Maduro's brutal dictatorship.

North Koreans have been under a brutal regime directly by the New World Order.

Europe is in shambles since the EU took over, and the migrants have flooded in.

Mexico is in utter ruin being tyrannized by drug lords.

Africa for years has continually had its assets stolen, not to mention the prolific evil of organ harvesting.

Until recently, Saudi Arabia was the head of worldwide human trafficking.

Most of the Middle East has held the people in untold oppression.

And America... oh dear, America. Under silent assault from every direction.

I didn't even mention the continual massive wars and all the deadly diseases.

So yes, the world has had tribulation upon tribulation.   I hope I never hear another person say in my lifetime that there has been no tribulation. Because it still rings in my ears and I'm shaking my head at the incredible deception! Thank the LORD this is all finally turning around! We are seeing the fulfillment of Daniel 8:25,

> *"And through his policy also he shall cause craft to prosper in his hand; he shall magnify himself in his heart, and by peace shall destroy many: he shall also stand up against the Prince of princes; but **he shall be broken without 'human' hand.**"*

Praise the LORD! We couldn't defeat the Beast, but our LORD – the STRONGER MAN - can!

> *"But if I cast out devils by the Spirit of God, then the kingdom of God is come unto you. Or else how can one enter into a strong man's house, and plunder his goods, except he first bind the strong man? and then he will plunder his house."* (Matthew 12:28-29)

Our LORD is our Stronger Man, and He is delivering the whole world from being held captive to satan!

ERROR # 9 EXPOSED -

There will be seven years of Worldwide Cataclysmic Tribulation. NO!

The New World Order minions infiltrated the seminaries and spread this error throughout the Church and entertainment. They said there is a remaining week in Daniel's prophecy that equates to seven years of worldwide catastrophic tribulation.

Most don't know that this widespread teaching comes from a very complex passage tucked in Daniel Chapter 9. We SHOULD NEVER build a super-structure of "End Times" or any other theology on an obscure passage filled with complicated symbolism. But that is EXACTLY what they did. See Chapter 5, "Tribulation Fake News", explaining Daniel 9.

ERROR # 10 EXPOSED -

The Anti-Christ Man of Lawlessness has not come yet. NO!

How would anyone recognize the Anti-Christ? Who gets to proclaim a person as the Anti-Christ? Check out this passage and then we can talk about it.

> *"The Day (Great Day of the LORD) will not come until the rebellion occurs and the **man of lawlessness (the son of destruction) is revealed.** He will oppose and exalt himself above every so-called god or object of worship. So he will seat himself in the temple of God, proclaiming himself to be God.*

*Do you not remember that I told you these things while I was still with you? And you know what is now restraining him, so that **he will be revealed at the proper time.** For the mystery of lawlessness is already at work, but the one who now restrains it will continue until he is taken out of the way. And **then the lawless one will be revealed,** whom the Lord Jesus will slay with the breath of His mouth and abolish by the majesty of His arrival.*

The coming of the lawless one will be accompanied by the working of satan, with every kind of power, sign, and false wonder, and with every wicked deception *directed against those who are perishing, because they refused the love of the truth that would have saved them. For this reason, God will send them a **powerful delusion** (Great Deception) so that they will believe the lie, in order that judgment will come upon all who have disbelieved the truth and delighted in wickedness."* (2nd Thessalonians 2)

So in this passage, the Lawless One is the Son of Destruction, aka Son of Perdition, aka Anti-Christ. ***He will be accompanied by the working of satan, with every kind of power, sign, and false wonder, and with every wicked deception.*** Who does that sound like to you?

All together now!

The New World Order Globalist Bloodlines!

We are not waiting for anyone to go sit in a temple. The Beast would never allow that! The Lawless One has been revealed. That is what the Great Awakening is all about. We know who our enemy is now. And that enemy is being destroyed! What a GREAT DAY!

The GREAT DECEPTION is referring to those who worked with the Beast (NWO) being deceived into doing evil and spreading lies and working injustice, in order to be rich and powerful. That is the GREAT DECEPTION. And they made a very, very bad choice. These past few years have given them one last opportunity to come out of this cabal before it is too late.

ERROR #11 EXPOSED -
The Name Jew Always Describes the Physical Lineage of Judah. The

Name Israel Always Describes the Physical Lineage of Jacob. NO!

When you read the word Israelite or Jew or Hebrew, sometimes the context is about the physical lineage, but many times it is talking about "God's family." Many believers are actually in the physical line of the Lost Tribes of Israel! Other believers have been adopted into God's family. Either way, believers from every nation are what the Bible calls **True Israelites... True Jews... True Hebrews...** the **True Family of God**. This is very important. The enemy has used the confusion about the word Jew and Israelite to cause unbelievable confusion.

> *"For he is not a Jew, which is one outwardly; neither is that circumcision, which is outward in the flesh: But he is a **Jew**, which is one **inwardly;** and circumcision is that **of the heart**, in the spirit, and not in the letter; whose praise is not of men, but of God."* (Romans 2:28-29)

> *"There is neither Jew nor Greek, there is neither bond nor free, there is neither male nor female: for you are all one in Christ Jesus. And if you be Christ's, then are you Abraham's seed, and heirs according to the promise."* (Galatians 3:28-29)

The LORD counts a Jew as someone who follows Him from their heart. Sadly there are many who claim to be Jews who do not follow the LORD, and are not physical Jews either, but have hijacked the name Jew for evil purposes.

ERROR # 12 EXPOSED -

"Fleeing into the mountains" verse is for future Tribulation. NO!

"When you therefore shall see the Abomination of Desolation, spoken of by Daniel the prophet, stand in the holy place, (whoso readeth, let him understand): Then let them which be in Judea flee into the mountains. Let him which is on the housetop not come down to take any thing out of his house. Neither let him which is in the field return back to take his clothes. And woe unto them that are with child, and to them that give suck in those days! But pray that your flight be not in the winter, neither on the sabbath day." (Matthew 24)

Jesus asked His disciples what they thought about those

buildings - namely the Temple in Jerusalem. And He warned them of those buildings' coming destruction. And it happened just as our LORD Jesus said it would. There was horrifying <u>abomination of desolation</u> committed in the temple, straight from the pits of hell. Just as we have learned about happening in tunnels underground. The Romans destroyed Jerusalem in A.D. 70. They pushed every stone off the temple mount to the ground far below. Not one stone was left on another. That is where the stones lay to this day. THAT is what Jesus was talking about in this passage. This event has already happened. This passage is NOT about a future event.

There are many gates to enter the literal City of Jerusalem. And symbolically, the gates of understanding have to be opened, for humanity to be free. Think of these errors I just listed as gates that were keeping us from finding the truth... from finding our way out of the matrix maze of deception, and finding our way to freedom. The gates are being opened, as in the passage,

> "Open wide, you gates. Open up, you ancient doors. Then the King of glory will come in!" (Psalm 24:7) and

> "I will build my church; and the gates of hell shall not prevail (stand) against it." (Matthew 16:18)

We are kicking those gates down, and NOTHING WILL STOP US!

I have exposed 12 common errors that we were told. Most of us have been deceived in a variety of ways. But guess what! God's Word promises that after the Beast and the False Prophet are cast into the abyss, satan will no longer deceive us! That is so hard to imagine, after having learned many of the ways we have been tricked, but all things are possible with God.

> "Then I saw an angel coming down from heaven with the key to the

*Abyss, holding in his hand a great chain. He seized the dragon, that ancient serpent who is the devil and satan, and bound him for a thousand years. And he threw him into the Abyss, shut it, and sealed it over him, so that **he could not deceive the nations until the thousand years** were complete."* (Revelation 20)

One of satan's most effective deception tools has been false prophets. We might think of those as primarily religious leaders, but that also includes false information of every kind... false educators - false reporters - false judges - false lawyers - false history - false science -

false doctors - false governments - false politicians - false wars - false food - false entertainment - false weather - false financial markets... anything false just won't stand up to our scrutiny. As we break into this new Deception-Free Age, day by day we are seeing that their lies just don't work any more. Imagine 10 years, and 20 without the lies! Our Awakening spells the end of the New World Order. Their rule over us will crumble as we see through the lies.

This is just the beginning!

We've been under a cloud of deception, and the sunlight of truth is finally starting to shine through!

One of the main reasons I am writing this book, is to hopefully bring more Christians into the fight. This is the Great Day to fight in the Battle of Armageddon, and most believers are missing it. Just like most of God's people missed it when Jesus came the first time!

If the Great Tribulation messages and movies have given you nightmares, you'll love the next chapter. The seven-year cataclysmic nuclear holocaust is FAKE NEWS!

CHAPTER 5

TRIBULATION FAKE NEWS

First and foremost, no matter what the correct interpretation is of this very complex and hidden passage in Daniel Chapter 9,

there will NOT be a seven-year cataclysmic nuclear holocaust tribulation to destroy the people of the earth. Period.

We know that, because our LORD is coming to RESCUE humanity from the Beast and False Prophet, NOT to DESTROY humanity! Spoiler alert! At the end of the book of Revelation, John shows us that the Beast and False Prophet are cast out! And then John shows us there will be peace on earth for 1,000 years. That promise is all throughout Scripture, as well as in the prayer our LORD taught us,

"Your kingdom come, Your will be done ON EARTH as it is in Heaven."

Even though the cataclysmic destruction of earth and its inhabitants is a widely-held view, **it is not correct**.

That false teaching comes in large part from a faulty interpretation of Daniel 9:27.

"And he shall confirm the covenant with many for one week: and in the midst of the week he shall cause the sacrifice and the oblation to cease, and for the overspreading of abominations he shall make it desolate."

The modern teaching is that the Anti-Christ is the one spoken of in verse 27 who will confirm a covenant with many for one week (seven years). I strongly disagree. The LORD Jesus is the one in this verse who confirms the covenant with His people.

Daniel was told, *"shut up the words, and seal the book, even to the time of the end."* (Daniel 12:4)

It is no surprise that these passages have been misinterpreted. God sealed them from our understanding, likely to throw off the enemy. But the time has finally come for these prophecies to be unsealed.

I will attempt to give my best understanding of this complex, misunderstood passage. As always, future will prove past.

In attempting again to "unseal" this passage, I have read and heard many interpretations. None have stood up to scrutiny. But as I was searching and asking the LORD to guide me (and my Freedom Force Battalion was praying also), I got some really good clues. I think I've got it! Or at least, I'm closer. As I mentioned before, in order to understand the prophecies, we MUST use our understanding not only of God's Word, but also of the Hebrew festivals and of Biblical astronomy. Here's what I discovered. First, let's read Daniel 9:24-26:

> 24 *"Seventy <u>weeks</u> are determined upon thy people and upon thy holy city, to finish the transgression, and to make an end of sins, and to make reconciliation for iniquity, and to bring in everlasting righteousness, and to seal up the vision and prophecy, and to anoint the most Holy.*
> 25 *Know therefore and understand, that from the going forth of the commandment to restore and to build Jerusalem unto the Messiah the Prince shall be <u>seven weeks,</u> and <u>threescore and two weeks</u>: the street shall be built again, and the wall, even in troublous times.*
> 26 *And after <u>threescore and two weeks</u> shall Messiah be cut off, but not for himself: and the people of the prince that shall come shall destroy the city and the sanctuary; and the end thereof shall be with a flood, and unto the end of the war desolations are determined."*

Notice the passage talks a lot about WEEKS. What should that remind us of? Those weeks are definitely NOT typical seven-day weeks. So what would an Israelite think of when they read "weeks"?

The Festival of Weeks! JUBILEE!!

The Festival of Weeks is celebrated during the seven weeks between Passover and Shavuot (Pentecost). During the "Festival of Weeks," each day, the omer (barley) is counted. After counting for seven weeks, a total of forty-nine days, the Day of Shavuot (Pentecost) arrives!

> *"From the day after the Sabbath—the day you bring the bundle of grain to be lifted up as a special offering—count off seven full weeks. Keep counting until the day after the seventh Sabbath, fifty days later. Then present an offering of new grain to the Lord."* (Leviticus 25:15-16)

There is a special celebration on the 50th day. We know that day as Pentecost, when the Holy Spirit was poured out on the disciples. This day represents blessing and plenty!

And get this! Every **seventh** Shavuot/Pentecost **everybody gets a vacation!** Remember "7" and vacation!

> *"For six years you may plant your fields and prune your vineyards and harvest your crops, but during **the seventh year the land must have a Sabbath year of complete rest.** It is the Lord's Sabbath."* (Leviticus 25:3-4)

Did you catch that? An entire year of vacation for everybody! The LORD set this up to prevent the criminals from enslaving the people. He does not intend for us to work our lives away. He wants us to LIVE! To have PLENTY! To have time to enjoy our families and not be a slave to any cabal!

And then... the Big Daddy Celebration of them all comes... **the JUBILEE!!** Check this one out!

> *"In addition, you must count off seven Sabbath years, **seven sets of seven years**, adding up to forty-nine years in all. Then on the Day of Atonement in the fiftieth year, blow the ram's horn loud and long throughout the land. Set this year apart as holy, a time to proclaim freedom throughout the land for all who live there."* (Leviticus 25:8-10)

Every 50 years, the Jubilee is to be celebrated! That means all debts are canceled, captives are freed, property returns to its original owner, and the land rests! Doesn't that sound wonderful?! Yes, it sounds amazing for the regular people who are in debt-slavery and under tyrannical oppression. But... sad to say, Jubilee has not been celebrated Biblically. Why didn't the Israelites observe Jubilee? The "elite" always kept everyone in debt slavery, and never allowed the Jubilee to be celebrated as the LORD prescribed. There was no way the big wigs would cancel the debts and return the property they had stolen! That was a major reason the people were taken captive into Babylon. The captivity <u>broke the power</u> of the "elite" in Jerusalem. When Daniel received this prophecy, the land of Jerusalem was at rest for 70 years because of all the prior years the Jubilee WAS NOT KEPT! So the LORD forced a sabbatical for the land.

So what does Jubilee have to do with the Daniel 9 prophecy? Remember how many times it said "weeks"?

SEVEN "WEEKS" IS A JUBILEE!

Did you catch that? That is a huge clue to unlocking Daniel 9! And we wouldn't clue into it, if we didn't know and keep the "Festival of Weeks"! So let's read the prophecy in light of understanding "weeks."

In verse 24, the LORD told Daniel there would be 70 "weeks" before the captives would return to Jerusalem. The LORD was talking about much more than just returning the captives in Babylon to Jerusalem. He was talking about <u>all of captive humanity being set free!</u>

Get what our LORD was saying. There would be

70 "weeks" = Ten Jubilees

to get rid of the evil empires that run the earth.

> *"Seventy weeks are determined upon thy people and upon thy holy city, to finish the transgression, and to make an end of sins, and to make reconciliation for iniquity, and to bring in everlasting righteousness, and to seal up the vision and prophecy, and to anoint the most Holy".*
> (Daniel 9:24)

At first glance, it looks like it would take 500 years for this prophecy to be fulfilled when the Messiah came. That was excruciating news for Daniel to take in. But we know the truth is that even when our Messiah came, that was not the end of the evil empires. Let's keep unlocking this mysterious prophecy. Regarding verse 24,

Did Jesus finish the transgression? Yes and no.
Did Jesus make an end of sins? Yes and no.
Did Jesus make reconciliation for iniquity? Yes and no.
Did Jesus bring in everlasting righteousness? Yes and no.
Did Jesus seal up the vision and prophecy? Yes and no.
Did Jesus anoint the most Holy? Yes.

Of course, I would never take anything away from what our LORD Jesus did on the cross. In a major way He accomplished all these promises above. But in His first mission, He did not destroy the evil tyrants who rule the earth. He did not assume His role as King and begin to reign on earth. He did not finish. He told us to go disciple the entire world. And when we were finished, we would kick out the Beast and False Prophet cabal together. That, my friends, is happening at the time of this writing! Promises Made. Promised Kept. KEK.

Next, let's break down verse 26 with the understanding of Jubilees and "weeks."

> *"Know therefore and understand, that from the going forth of the commandment to restore and to build Jerusalem unto the Messiah the Prince shall be seven weeks, and threescore and two weeks: the street shall be built again, and the wall, even in troublous times."*

NOTE: For clarification, here is the same verse, but I re-ordered the numbers of weeks in verse 26, respective to the nouns they modify:

> *"Know therefore and understand, that from the going forth of the commandment to restore and to build Jerusalem shall be seven weeks, and unto the Messiah the Prince, threescore and two weeks (62 weeks):"*

What if the first "seven weeks" (seven "7"s) was the first Jubilee to be celebrated after the Babylonian captives returned to Jerusalem and rebuilt the city?

And then the Messiah would enter Jerusalem after nine more Jubilees (63 weeks = 9 "7"'s)?

45

Remember,
"Festival of Weeks" = **Annual Spring Harvest Celebration** = **"Festival of Firstfruits"** = **"Counting of Omer"** for 49 days from Passover to Pentecost (aka Shavuot) on the 50th day.

a **"WEEK"** = 7 **"Festival of Weeks"** = **7-year period** = **"7"** = **"Vacation"**

a **"JUBILEE"** = 7 **"WEEKS"** (7 7-year periods) = **"50"** = **50th Year** = **Restoration**

Here is a chart of the 10 Jubilees in Daniel's prophecy:

7 "WEEKS" (1 7-yr period)   70 "WEEKS"

63 "WEEKS" (9 7-yr periods)	(10 JUBILEES)	CELEBRATE?	EST. YEAR
		Edict to Rebuild	~467 BC
Edict Marker = 7 "weeks"	Jubilee 1	Nehemiah's Jubilee	~417 BC
*1st "7" = 7 "weeks"	Jubilee 2	NO JUBILEE	367 BC
+ 2nd "7"= 14 "weeks"	Jubilee 3	NO JUBILEE	317 BC
+ 3rd "7" = 21 "weeks"	Jubilee 4	NO JUBILEE	267 BC
+ 4th "7" = 28 "weeks"	Jubilee 5	NO JUBILEE	217 BC
+ 5th "7" = 35 "weeks"	Jubilee 6	NO JUBILEE	167 BC
+ 6th "7" = 42 "weeks"	Jubilee 7	NO JUBILEE	117 BC
+ 7th "7" = 49 "weeks"	Jubilee 8	NO JUBILEE	67 BC
+ 8th "7" = 56 "weeks"	Jubilee 9	NO JUBILEE	17 BC
+ 9th "7" = 63 "weeks"	Jubilee 10	JESUS CUT OFF	33 AD

The more I think about it, the more I'm sure "weeks" in Daniel 9 MUST be talking about Jubilee "weeks." It might take a minute for us to wrap our heads around the terminology of "weeks" and Jubilees. But it is very important, and was intended to protect us from the cabal. Here is what the LORD said His purpose for these festivals is:

> *"If you want to live securely in the land, follow my decrees and obey my regulations. Then the land will yield large crops, and you will eat your fill and live securely in it."* (Leviticus 25:18-19)

If the people had kept Jubilee, the tyrants would never have gotten a foothold. The people would have never become enslaved. I feel like a kid who didn't pay attention when my mom told me not to touch the hot stove. Humanity should have listened... and obeyed. Instead we all became slaves.

So, back to Daniel 9.

> *"And after threescore and two weeks (62 weeks)* shall Messiah be cut off, *but not for himself: and the people of the prince that shall come shall destroy the city and the sanctuary;"*

What if Jesus was "cut off" from celebrating Jubilee, and he was stopped from setting the people free from the tyrants? I think we are onto something! It would not surprise me that the power players killed Jesus to stop the Jubilee. I bet the government and religious leaders thought Jesus was going to fulfill Daniel 9! They thought He would restore to the people everything the "elite" had stolen from them! They would never allow that! So Jesus was killed on Passover, only 50 days shy of Pentecost/Shavuot. This would have been the 10th Jubilee, as foretold in Daniel 9.

Jesus entered Jerusalem in the Triumphal Entry ready to take His power and rule, but the people were not ready to take down the evil rulers, and Jesus knew it. Jesus was cut off (crucified) before He could set the people free. He knew this was the plan from the beginning, and that is why He set us to work making disciples to the uttermost part of the world. Instead of setting the people of Jerusalem free, Jesus sent the Holy Spirit on Pentecost to infill and empower the disciples to begin to set the whole world free!

What does the prophecy say happens next? It says,

> *"the people of the prince that shall come shall destroy the city and the sanctuary".*

The evildoers (people of the prince of the power of the air) would destroy the city, the temple, whatever they had to destroy, so no one could ever celebrate the Jubilee! They will destroy everything to keep the masses enslaved and their power intact.

With what we know about the evil empire cabal, that sounds EXACTLY RIGHT!

Ok... ready for verse 27? This one is going to be out there. Here it is:

> *"And he shall confirm the covenant with many for one week: and in the midst of the week he shall cause the sacrifice and the oblation to cease, and for the overspreading of abominations he shall make it desolate, even until the consummation, and that determined shall be poured upon the desolate."*

This is the verse that is interpreted by mainstream teachers, that the "Anti-Christ" will confirm a covenant, or a treaty, with many, which will usher in a seven-year cataclysmic nuclear holocaust tribulation. **That is false.**

Let's consider the verse this way:

The LORD Jesus is the one who confirms the covenant for one week. How might our Lord confirm the covenant? A covenant is an agreement between two or more persons. What agreement has He made with us?   He promised that, at the end of the age (2,000 year period), He would rule the earth and kick out the Beast and False Prophet! Well, how might He confirm this? Maybe...

THE GREAT AWAKENING OF HUMANITY???!!!

I don't know about you, but I'm feeling that confirmation right about now! Seeing people all over the world rising up to destroy the New World Order, is no doubt a confirmation of His covenant promise to us!

But why does he "confirm the covenant with many for one week?" (seven years) Because He is now finishing what He started 2,000 years ago.   Jesus was cut off before He finished celebrating Jubilee, setting the world free, thereby destroying the schemes of the controllers and their abuse of the people. So now He is finishing that week and will celebrate Jubilee, whether the cabal likes it or not!

At the time I am writing this, we are half-way through the

"week", the seven-year period that started on the Feast of Trumpets, which kicked off the worldwide Great Awakening. Soon the NWO will be devastated, and our healing and restoration will take off like a rocket!

Now check the last part of verse 27.

> "and in the midst of the week he shall cause the sacrifice and the oblation to cease,"

Do you know what that means? Before the Great Awakening, I had no idea about the horrifying ritual sacrifices and satanic worship going on underneath our feet. I thought this verse was talking about stopping the sacrifices and worship in Jerusalem, when the temple was destroyed in A.D. 70. But do you want to know what I think this verse is referring to? When is the "midst (middle) of the week"? Three and one half years. What happened three and a half years after the Great Awakening began at the Feast of Trumpets, October 2, 2016? The children in underground tunnels were rescued and the ritual sacrifices and satanic worship were stopped worldwide! With our President giving us clues like, "There is light at the end of the tunnel," we feel confident this is true! Our LORD Jesus "caused the satanic sacrifice and oblation to cease!" Praise the LORD!

We know the evil power of the cabal has been broken. Their empire is crumbling. And, guess what else. This verse tells exactly what the LORD will do to these evildoers. As verse 27 says,

> "for the overspreading of abominations he shall make it desolate, even until the consummation, and that determined shall be poured upon the desolate."

In other words, because of the abject evil they have committed, God will pour out His wrath on the New World Order, and they will be made desolate... empty... destroyed... devastated.

This interpretation satisfies every part of the Daniel 9 prophecy and is also in alignment with Revelation and the other prophecies. It is confirmed by the Hebrew festivals. And of course, the clarity of understanding is due to the Great Awakening and our wonderful "you-know-who."   Each day things will become clearer and future will prove past.

No doubt the LORD wants us to focus on "weeks" and Jubilees... and to CELEBRATE!

By the way, there is an entire ancient text called "The Book of Jubilees" in which the LORD tracks time in Jubilees. It's like counting history by 50's.

We're almost ready to dive into the Book of Revelation. Before we do, let's go over some helpful tips on understanding this complex, symbolic part of God's Word.

CHAPTER 6
REVELATION TIPS

C onfession time. Until the past few years, I've never paid much attention to the Book of Revelation. I pretty much ignored it. It intimidated me, I guess... but mostly, I just didn't feel the need to focus on it. Maybe because the various popular views left me looking for another menu. Maybe because it seemed really controversial. As if to say, "If these people who spend all their time on this subject have so many competing views, why should I even try?! It's obviously waaaay too complicated." Maybe because even though I knew the verse that said the reader of Revelation would be blessed, I was led to believe, as many do, that I should stay away from it. But the recent events have made me wonder if something REALLY HUGE IS HAPPENING.

BIG.

BIGGER.

BIGGEST.

So I began to search diligently for answers. I have been researching, and studying, focusing on the pertinent Scriptures, and reading other Bible passages in a whole new light.

Our LORD Jesus said,

> "If you will not watch, I will come upon you as a thief, and you will not know what hour I will come upon you." (Revelation 3:3)

It's time to know, y'all.

I don't want to miss this. Many are completely unaware that this is the Great Day of the LORD... because they are not WATCHING, as He told us to. So let's research, and ask the LORD to guide us... and watch, everyone!

Though I've listened to various teachers on the Revelation, I felt that I mostly should listen to the LORD'S impressions on me, as I dug. If I'm wrong about a few things, it's not the end of the world... hahaha... get it?

(That's a little "End Times" humor, in case you missed it.) By the way, End Times means End of the AGE (2,000 year period), not THE END OF TIME.

HELPFUL TIPS

1. When I first began studying the Book of Revelation, I took some great advice, and I read it completely through three times. And I wrote down verse by verse, in my own words, what I thought each verse meant. (Actually the best thing I did to get a better understanding of the Revelation was that I started at the end... and worked backwards! We'll get to that.)

2. Revelation is funny. It isn't chronological. John gives the Revelation in lots of short stories, from beginning to end, and then retells the story from a different vantage point. So you get a short version, a medium version, and a long version, repeating the story, to lock it into our minds. I think it's unwise to force-fit Revelation into chronological order. That's one reason why there is so much confusion out there.

3. John stops and focuses on the major players - the 144,000, and the Beast, the False Prophet, the Harlot, and the 24 Elders, in more detail. It's quite a star-studded cast of good and evil.

4. John also stops and tells us what is going on in Heaven, behind the scenes. It is eye-opening to realize that this epic event is taking place on earth AND in Heaven!

5. The imagery and symbolism is overwhelming! Especially at first, until you get a handle on the players. When in doubt, likely

the passage is symbolic.

6. Revelation expects the reader to be an avid Bible student. He expects the reader to know the Hebrew festivals inside and out. John uses stories and imagery from all over God's Word. So, we have to use the whole Bible to interpret the Revelation.

7.   Revelation expects that the reader understands the heavenly signs in the Mazzaroth (the Biblical word for the constellations or Zodiac). That's hugely important, and was common knowledge throughout all the centuries, until we got so intelligent in this modern day. (another joke) Daniel knew all about how the LORD speaks through the constellations. The heavens really do speak the glory and the story of God! That's how Daniel taught the Wise Men, who 600 years later, knew by the stars, that Jesus Christ was being born. As Genesis 1:14 says:

> *"And God said, Let there be lights in the firmament of the heaven to divide the day from the night; and let them be for **SIGNS**, and for seasons, and for days, and years."*

8.   The overarching theme of the Revelation is "JESUS is the King of the World," "He is setting up His earthly kingdom," and "Believers will reign with Him." Keep that in mind and you've got Revelation licked!

Intimidated yet? Fools rush in where angels fear to tread, so let's go!

With those thoughts in mind, here are brief summaries of some of the first chapters of the Revelation.

CHAPTER 7
REVELATION'S 7 STARS

T he purpose of this book is to focus on the Great Awakening and the Battle of Armageddon. I'm not really trying to write a book specifically explaining the Book of the Revelation. And I do not want to get bogged down with identifying each and every detail. So I will just give a brief summary of the first six chapters of the Book of Revelation and we can focus our attention on the Great Awakening and casting the Beast and False Prophet into the Abyss!!! Hoooah!

I'm tempted to post each and every verse here, but then I might as well paste in the entire Bible! LOL! So I will give you precious nuggets that focus on this Epic Battle we are fighting!

> *"And has made us **kings and priests** unto God and his Father; to him be glory and dominion for ever and ever. Amen."* (Revelation 1:6)

What an honor to be His ambassador on earth to bring light through the Government and the Church!

> *"Behold, he comes with clouds; and every eye shall see him, and they also which pierced him: and all kindred of the earth shall wail because of him. Even so, Amen."* (Revelation 1:9)

His appearing is a fearful thing for the disobedient. Remember, "clouds" is a symbolic term for coming in great power. For those of His who "love His appearing" (2nd Timothy 4), we say, "Even so, come!"

> *"I ...heard behind me a great voice, as of a trumpet, Saying, I am Alpha and Omega, the first and the last: and, What you see, write in a book, and send it unto the seven churches ...I saw seven golden candlesticks; ...And in the midst of the seven candlesticks one like unto the Son of man, clothed with a garment down to the foot, and girt*

about the waist with a golden girdle… His head and his hairs were white like wool, as white as snow; and his eyes were as a flame of fire; And his feet like unto fine brass, as if they burned in a furnace; and his voice as the sound of many waters.

And he had in his right hand seven stars: and out of his mouth went a sharp two-edged sword: and his countenance was as the sun shines in his strength. And when I saw him, I fell at his feet as dead. And he laid his right hand upon me, saying unto me, Fear not; I am the first and the last: I am he that lives, and was dead; and, behold, I am alive for evermore, Amen; and have the keys of hell and of death." (Revelation 1 excerpts)

Our Wonderful LORD Jesus is the King of the World, and He is our Best Friend. He holds the keys of hell and death. He wants us to know what will happen… and comforts us by saying, "Do not Fear."

The seven stars, which we will see in later chapters, represent the Church, which are meant to light the world. Check out in the picture below of the seven churches in Asia Minor - which is modern day Turkey. Notice how these seven churches form the very same shape as

Pleiades – in the heart of Taurus the bull. Taurus represents Jesus coming on a rampage to destroy the NWO Beast! I don't think it is a coincidence that the seven churches of Revelation form the same shape as Pleiades in Taurus' heart!

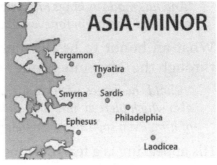

How cool is that?! (more on that in Revelation 15!)

To Ephesus He says,

"I know your works, and your labor, and your patience, and how you can not bear them which are evil: and you have tried them which say they are apostles, and are not, and have found them liars:

And have suffered patiently, and for my name's sake have labored, and have not fainted." (Revelation 2:2-3)

That section brings tears to my eyes. Our LORD KNOWS how we fight day after day against this evil, and how we have found out who are liars, and that we try to expose them and fight for justice. He is very proud of us for fighting hard and not giving up.

> *"I know your works, and tribulation, and poverty, (but remember, you are rich!) and I know the blasphemy of them which say they are Jews, and are not, but are the synagogue of satan."* (Revelation 2:10)

He knows everything we have been through at the hands of these demon-possessed criminals, and how they have hijacked the name Jew for evil purposes.

> *"Beware them that hold the doctrine of Balaam, who taught to eat ritual sacrifices, and to commit sexual perversion."* (Revelation 2:14)

We've read this so many times, but didn't realize until the Great Awakening that Jesus was telling us about a worldwide criminal pedo mafia!

> *"Do not allow... to teach and to seduce my servants to commit fornication, and to eat ritual sacrifices."* (Revelation 2:20)

How could we have missed this?!! He warned us, but most of us could never imagine this was being done in our day!

> *"Hold fast till I come. He that overcomes, and keeps my works unto the end, to him will I give power over the nations: And he shall rule them with a rod of iron; as the vessels of a potter shall they be broken to shivers: even as I received of my Father. And I will give him the morning star.* (Venus which symbolizes love)
>
> *He that has an ear, let him hear what the Spirit says unto the churches."* (Revelation 2:25-29)

We are holding on, overcoming, keeping His words, and helping Him smash their evil kingdom to bits! He gives us His great love... and His smile, which is worth more than diamonds! He has given us ears to hear, and eyes to see what is going on! Thank You LORD for this honor!

> *"I know your works, that you have a name that you live, and are dead. Be watchful, and strengthen the things which remain, that are ready to die: Remember therefore what you have received and heard, and*

hold firmly, and repent. If therefore you shall not watch, I will come on you as a thief, and you shalt not know what hour I will come upon you." (Revelation 3)

This speaks volumes to the modern church. They look alive... but are asleep... some groups are dying... some are stone-cold dead. Jesus is not talking about numbers. He's talking about His people who are supposed to light the darkness! But many of His people are in the dark about these evils going on right under their noses!

He said if we are not watching, He will come as a thief. But if we watch, we will recognize His appearing!

"Behold, I will make them of the synagogue of satan, which say they are Jews, and are not, but do lie; behold, I will make them to come and worship before your feet, and to know that I have loved thee." (Revelation 3:9)

Get ready! The fake Jews, who say they are God's people, who have lied, and stolen, and done untold crimes against humanity, will soon have to admit that WE are truly God's people, whom He loves!

*"Him that overcomes will I make a pillar in the temple of my God, and he shall go no more out: and I will write upon him the name of my God, and the name of the city of my God, which is new Jerusalem, which comes down out of heaven from my God: and **I will write upon him my new name.**"* (Revelation 3:12)

So many blessings are coming! I love this one in particular! He will write on us **HIS NEW NAME**! Wonder what THAT NAME is! I think I know. I'm not saying yet.

"I know your works, that you are neither cold nor hot: I would you were cold or hot. Because you are lukewarm, and neither cold nor hot, I will spew you out of my mouth." (Rev. 3:15)

May He NEVER have cause to say this to any one of us!

"As many as I love, I rebuke and chasten: be zealous therefore, and repent. Behold, I stand at the door, and knock: if any man hear my voice, and open the door, I will come in to him, and will sup with him, and he with me. To him that overcomes will I grant to sit with me in my throne, even as I also overcame, and am set down with my Father in his

throne." (Rev. 3:19-21)

We have heard His voice.

We have opened the door.

He spends time with us daily.

We overcome! And we will rule with Him!

Four Living Creatures

There are so many remarkable things to point out in Chapter 4, but I'm going to just point out my thoughts on the Four Beasts. We will see them later in Revelation too. What in the world could they represent?!

> 6 *"In the midst of the throne, and round about the throne, were* **four beasts full of eyes before and behind.**
>
> 7 *And the first beast was like a* **lion**, *and the second beast like a* **calf (ox)**, *and the third beast had a* **face as a man**, *and the fourth beast was like* **a flying eagle**.
>
> 8 *And the four beasts had each of them six wings about him; and they were full of eyes within: and they rest* not day and *night,* **saying, Holy, holy, holy, Lord God Almighty, which was, and is, and is to come."** (Revelation 4:7-8)

First off, these are NOT the same creatures of Revelation 13, or in Daniel's visions. These Beings do NOT represent tyrannical world empires. They are NOT another created being, because the LORD has told us all the types of creatures He made.

Check out this image of Israel's camp in the wilderness, surrounding the Tabernacle, which housed the Ark of the Covenant. The four primary flags of Israel that faced the Tabernacle were a **Lion**, an **Ox**, a **Man**, and an **Eagle**! That's it! The four Living Creatures represent us! God's people, turned to worship Him! Mystery Solved!

I just love it when we unlock the beautiful mysteries of God's Word!

Further, these four point us to the four Gospels God's people carry to the world.

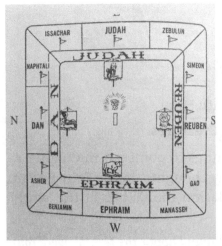

Matthew like a Lion: This Gospel highlights Christ's Kingly Authority and Judgment.

Mark like an Ox: This Gospel highlights Christ's Servanthood and Workmanship.

Luke like a Man: This Gospel highlights Christ's Humanity and Compassion.

John like an Eagle: This Gospel highlights Christ's Strength by the Spirit of God.

And how do we accomplish this monumental task of sharing these Gospels? Day and night, we do not stop speaking of His great wisdom ("full of eyes"), proclaiming the LORD is Holy, Holy, HOLY.

Summary of these first chapters of Revelation:

-Revelation started with our LORD Jesus giving us comfort, reminding us not to be afraid.

-Then warned us to fight, Fight, FIGHT against the evil empire.

-Then reminded us of the Great Rewards we will enjoy.

-And then gave us a glimpse of the breath-taking worship of Christ, from every creature, and from the very Gospels in the Word of God that tell the world of His great promises and love!

All that's left is to get this show on the road, and kick the Evil Empire into the Abyss! But therein is the problem. Who can get this started?

"And I saw a strong angel proclaiming with a loud voice, Who is worthy to open the book, and to loose the seals thereof?" (Revelation 5:2)

"But no one in heaven or on earth or under the earth was able to open the scroll and read it. Then I began to weep bitterly because no one was found worthy to open the scroll and read it. But one of the twenty-four elders said to me," (Rev 5:3-4)

*"**Stop weeping**! Look, the Lion of the tribe of Judah, the heir to David's throne, has won the victory. **He is worthy to open the scroll and its seven seals.**"* (**Revelation 5:5**)

Praise the LORD! He alone is worthy to open the seals! Only He is able to defeat the Evil Empire! So many have tried and failed. But this time, the LORD will open the seals, because only He has the combination to crack the code of evil that has held us in chains. It seems like it has taken so long, and we've only been in this battle since October 2017. The Team has planned this for 20 years! No matter how long it takes, it will be done according to the LORD'S plan. This time, we will *"escape as a bird out of the snare of the fowlers."* (Psalm 124:7)

Oh, and did you notice that verse is Revelation **5:5**?

9 *"And they sang a new song, saying, **You are worthy to take the book, and to open the seals thereof:** for you were slain, and have redeemed us to God by your blood out of every kindred, and tongue, and people, and nation;*

10 And have made us unto our God kings and priests: and we shall reign on the earth.

11 And I beheld, and I heard the voice of many angels round about the throne and the beasts and the elders: and the number of them was ten thousand times ten thousand, and thousands of thousands;

12 Saying with a loud voice, Worthy is the Lamb that was slain to receive power, and riches, and wisdom, and strength, and honor, and glory, and blessing." (Revelation 5:9-12)

What jumped out at you in that passage? Here's what jumped out at me... Jesus has redeemed us for an amazing purpose!

So we will be kings and priests and reign with Him on the earth!

What a high calling we have! We have been pushed to the side by the enemy for so long, but not for much longer! Put that on your refrigerator door, so you will never forget the wonderful future the LORD has planned for us! Because of Christ, we can go to the next chapter, in complete confidence that THIS WILL HAPPEN. We will be set free from the NWO satanists! Jesus is the Victor over the enemy!

He will Reign Forever! And we will reign with Him!

If you've read this far, it's likely because you are wiping the sleepy of deception out of your eyes! Now, let's splash some water on our faces!

CHAPTER 8
CONQUERING HORSES

In Revelation Chapter 6, John wrote that four horsemen were released - persecuting believers and wreaking all kinds of death and destruction on earth! (I personally am over it.) And then in verses 12-17, John fast-forwards to the time when the Beast is exposed and destroyed by the LORD! We are only in Chapter 6! WOW! That IS a short story!
(See what I mean? Revelation is not chronological!)

Revelation 6
> 1 "And I saw when the Lamb opened one of the seals, and I heard, as it were the noise of thunder, one of the four beasts saying, Come and see. 2 And I saw, and behold a **white horse**: and he that sat on him had a bow; and a crown was given unto him: and he went forth conquering, and to **conquer**."

The white horse represents the Fake Christ, "the Anti-Christ" who claims to be the champion of the people, but is actually conquering the unsuspecting masses.

> 3 "And when he had opened the second seal, I heard the second beast say, Come and see.
> 4 And there went out another **horse that was red**: and power was given to him that sat thereon to **take peace from the earth,** and that they should kill one another: and there was given unto him a great sword."

The red horse represents war. War is a huge Money Maker for the New World Order. With unspeakably terrible suffering and death. Just exactly what makes hell shriek with hideous delight.

> 5 "And when he had opened the third seal, I heard the third beast say, Come and see. And I beheld, and lo a **black horse**; and he that sat on him had a **pair of balances** in his hand.
> 6 And I heard a voice in the midst of the four beasts say, A measure of

> *wheat for a penny, and three measures of barley for a penny; and see thou hurt not the oil and the wine."*

The black horse brings starvation and deprivation. Think Central Banks... monopoly money... taxes, and theft of a nations' sources. The NWO certainly does not *need* our assets. They actually take pleasure in our suffering. Fretting over a drop of oil! Even though we've suffered, God's people are protected from evil.

> 7 *"And when he had opened the fourth seal, I heard the voice of the fourth beast say, Come and see.*
>
> 8 *And I looked, and behold a **pale horse**: and his name that sat on him was **Death, and Hell** followed with him. And power was given unto them over the fourth part of the earth, to kill with sword, and with hunger, and with death, and with the beasts of the earth.*
>
> 9 *And when he had opened the fifth seal, I saw under the altar the souls of them that were slain for the word of God, and for the testimony which they held:*
>
> 10 *"And they cried with a loud voice, saying, **How long, O Lord, holy and true, do you not judge and avenge our blood on them that dwell on the earth?**"*

The pale horse has brought untold misery and death in more ways than I care to enumerate. We are all crying out with a loud voice, "How long, LORD?"

> 11 *"And white robes were given unto every one of them; and it was said unto them, that they should rest yet for a little season, until their fellow servants also and their brethren, that should be killed as they were, should be fulfilled.*
>
> 12 *And I beheld when he had opened the sixth seal, and, lo, there was a great earthquake; and the sun became black as sackcloth of hair, and the moon became as blood."*

I think the earthquake is more about exposing their crimes, rather than a physical geological earthquake.

Blood Moons and Eclipses are Warning signs to the New World Order, like flashing lights in the heavens! Just take a look at how many we have had recently!

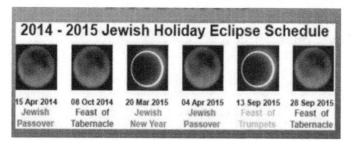

13 "The stars of heaven fell unto the earth, even as a fig tree casts her untimely figs, when she is shaken of a mighty wind."

Sounds like Movie Stars – the rich and famous dropping like figs.

*14 "Heaven departed as **a scroll when it is rolled together;** and every mountain and island were moved out of their places."*

Chemtrails look a lot like scrolls rolled together. Just sit and watch the sky sometime, and you will see cloud-scrolls filling the sky! The LORD knew they would use every bit of technology to try to destroy us.

The mountains represent the powerful. The islands represent the weak. They are all being shaken to their core as their crimes are being exposed.

15 "And the kings of the earth, and the great men, and the rich men, and the chief captains, and the mighty men, and every bondman, and every free man, hid themselves in the dens and in the rocks of the mountains;

*16 And said to the **mountains and rocks, Fall on us, and hide us from the face of him that sits on the throne, and from the wrath of the Lamb**."*

Sounds like bunkers to me! And all the panic the NWO is experiencing as they try to keep their crimes hidden. There is nowhere to run and nowhere to hide!

17 "For the great day of his wrath is come; and who shall be able to stand?"

Only the righteous will stand. The satan worshipers will fall like a stone!

Wow! The whole story of Revelation in **17** verses! How did we finish so fast? We're not finished yet. John will tell the Revelation in a variety of ways. Buckle up for the next telling of God's Victory over our enemies!

CHAPTER 9
KNIGHTHOOD

On to Revelation Chapter 7...

The first thing we see is four angels standing on the four corners of the earth, holding back the four winds.

*1 "And after these things I saw **four angels standing on the four corners of the earth, holding the four winds** of the earth, that the wind should not blow on the earth, nor on the sea, nor on any tree."*

Why are these angels standing there holding back the winds of the earth?

2nd Thessalonians 2:8 gives us a clue.

*6 "And you know what is **holding him back,** for he can be revealed only when his time comes. 7 For this lawlessness is already at work secretly, and **it will remain secret** until the one who is holding it back steps out of the way."*

The world en masse was not ready to know the truth. To be honest, none of us were really ready to swallow these horrible redpills. We choked them down because we are the Patriots. The four angels have been holding back these secrets for thousands of years. Then when it was time, the angels blew this truth into us. They revealed these hard truths to us, and gathered us together to fight. Each one of us who has awakened knows that one day these secrets were hidden, and then the angels woke us up, just like Mark 13 told us would happen.

26 "then shall they see the Son of man coming in the clouds with great power and glory

*27 And then shall he send **his angels, and shall gather together his*** *elect from the four winds, from the uttermost part of the earth to the uttermost part of heaven."*

and Isaiah 11:12 *"And he shall set up an **ensign** for the nations, and shall assemble the outcasts of Israel, and **gather together the dispersed of Judah from the four corners** of the earth."*

And Ezekiel told us the same thing! Remember Chapter 37 when Ezekiel was told to "prophesy to the wind"?

*"Prophesy unto the wind, prophesy, son of man, and say to the wind, Thus said the Lord God; **Come from the four winds**, O breath, and breathe upon these slain, that they may live."*

That is exactly what John is describing too! They both saw this Day of Great Awakening when the winds of truth would blow into our ears all over the earth! And humanity would rise from the dead, figuratively speaking, of course.

The verse in Revelation goes on to say that **the wind should not blow** until every single warrior of the 144,000 in the Army of God was sealed.

Revelation 7

*1 "And after these things I saw four angels standing on the **four corners** of the earth, holding the four winds of the earth, that **the wind should not blow on the earth, nor on the sea, nor on any tree.***

2 And I saw another angel ascending from the east, having the seal of the living God: and he cried with a loud voice to the four angels, to whom it was given to hurt the earth and the sea,

*3 Saying, Hurt not the earth, neither the sea, nor the trees, till we have **sealed the servants of our God in their foreheads."***

The angel in the east told the four angels not to HURT THE EARTH or SEA or TREES. That has made this section very confusing. I think that "disinformation" was necessary, to keep this a secret from the enemy.

The angels are not going to HURT the earth. They are going to reveal some very PAINFUL TRUTHS to the servants/warriors. We have to know the truth, no matter how much it hurts to know. But with that knowledge, also comes the seal and protection and understanding from God, so we can "handle the truth."

With this seal, we have been "knighted" to be God's elite forces. Ordained by God for this very important task. Kind of like the SEALs special operations forces in the US Military!

The seal is our armor that equips and protects us moment by moment as we fight this battle. We are reminded how we are not fighting flesh and blood, but spiritual forces, and we MUST use our heavenly armor. In order to stand our ground, we need God's power and protection... the breastplate of RIGHTEOUSNESS, the helmet of SALVATION, the belt of TRUTH, shoes of PEACE, the Sword of the Spirit- the WORD of GOD, the shield of FAITH, and constant PRAYER. Boy do we need it! The surprise attacks come from all directions. It's so great that we have our Patriots, with posts periodically, helping us stay together and focused.

In ancient times, the king's wax seal meant no one could tamper with the item on penalty of death. Same goes for us! Those who fight on God's side are spiritually bullet-proof! We have the mind of Christ on our foreheads! This is **NOT** a physical mark, of course. But everyone knows those who stand up and fight for the Kingdom of Christ in this battle, even without a physical mark.

> 4 "And I heard the number of them which were sealed: and there were sealed **a hundred and forty and four thousand** of all the tribes of the children of Israel. 5 Of the tribe of _Judah_ were sealed twelve thousand. Of the tribe of _Reuben_ were sealed twelve thousand. Of the tribe of _Gad_ were sealed twelve thousand. 6 Of the tribe of _Asher_ were sealed twelve thousand. Of the tribe of _Nephthali_ were sealed twelve thousand. Of the tribe of _Manasses_ were sealed twelve thousand. 7 Of the tribe of _Simeon_ were sealed twelve thousand. Of the tribe of _Levi_ were sealed twelve thousand. Of the tribe of _Issachar_ were sealed twelve thousand. 8 Of the tribe of _Zebulon_ were sealed twelve thousand. Of the tribe of _Joseph_ were sealed twelve thousand. Of the tribe of _Benjamin_ were sealed twelve thousand."

So who are the 12,000 from each tribe of Israel?

These 144,000 Israelites represent the warriors/SEALs/Knights/

special forces who were gathered by the four angels. All fighting for justice and freedom. True Israelites in heart. Some from the Lost Tribes of Israel. Some who have been adopted into God's family. Either way, they are all Abraham's seed in their hearts, without regard to their nationality or creed.

> "And if you be Christ's, then are you Abraham's seed, and heirs according to the promise." (Galatians 3)

> "But he is a Jew, which is one inwardly; and circumcision is that of the heart, in the spirit, and not in the letter." (Romans 2:29)

These servants of God have been chosen to fight on the front lines in this Great Battle of Armageddon. Good versus Evil. The 12,000 x 12 = 144,000 is not about an EXACT number, but about a PERFECT number. Exactly the individuals whom the LORD planned to fight in this battle. We will talk about them more in Revelation Chapter 14.

Interestingly, the tribes of Dan and Ephraim are not mentioned in the list of tribes. The tribe of Dan actually moved into Ephraim's territory, so they are listed together as the tribe of Joseph. Dan's symbol is an eagle, which is most assuredly where America's national symbol came from. Ephraim's symbol is a bull, and his brother, Manasseh's symbols are olive branches and arrows, just like on the Presidential seal. No doubt many of our forefathers were from these tribes and they left the codes for us.

> 9 "After this I beheld, and, lo, **a great multitude**, which no man could number, of all nations, and kindred, and people, and tongues, stood before the throne, and before the Lamb, clothed with white robes, and palms in their hands."

So who is this great multitude/innumerable group - all dressed in white, "having washed their robes in the blood of the lamb?" This is the entire group who put their faith in Christ since the beginning of time. They love the LORD. They honor Him in their lives. But they were not chosen to be one of the 144,000 Knights.

> 10 "And cried with a loud voice, saying, Salvation to our God which sits

upon the throne, and unto the Lamb.

11 And all the angels stood round about the throne, and about the elders and the four beasts, and fell before the throne on their faces, and worshiped God,

12 Saying, Amen: Blessing, and glory, and wisdom, and thanksgiving, and honor, and power, and might, be unto our God for ever and ever. Amen.

13 And one of the elders answered, saying unto me, **What are these which are arrayed in white robes? and whence came they?**

14 And I said unto him, Sir, you know. And he said to me, These are they which came out of **great tribulation***, and have washed their robes, and made them white in the blood of the Lamb."*

All these came out of great tribulation. So what is this great tribulation? We will talk about that more too, but it is not what we were led to believe. The great tribulation is NOT the nuclear destruction and obliteration of all of humanity.

Great tribulation is the suffering of humanity <u>for all time</u> under the evil empires. But this final New World Order evil empire has caused worse suffering and deception than all the former empires did.

The great multitude mentioned in verse 9, are true believers of all time. They have been victorious, refusing to participate in the evil satanic rituals and lawlessness of the Beast.

The 144,000 warriors are finally fighting the Battle of Armageddon. We will be victorious and cast the Beast and False Prophet into the abyss!

Here are prophecies about the final part of the great tribulation. This prophecy from Daniel 8 tells us about the New World Order run by satanic deceptive power.

"And in the latter time of their kingdom **(last of the kingdoms/ empires in Chapter 8)***, when the transgressors are come to the full, a king of fierce countenance, and understanding dark sentences* **(satanic)***, shall stand up.*

24 And his power shall be mighty, but not by his own power **(satanic power)***: and he shall destroy wonderfully* **(shockingly)***, and shall* *prosper, and practice, and shall **destroy** the mighty and the holy people.*

25 And through his policy also he shall cause craft **(deceit/trickery/ deception)** *to prosper in his hand; and he shall magnify himself in his heart* **(absolute pride)**, *and by peace shall **destroy** many."* (Daniel 8)

This is the DECEPTION the New World Order has used against us, which will be destroyed. We see their power to deceive is breaking down even now! Praise the LORD! Notice it says the holy people were DESTROYED. But as Revelation 11 says, BY GOD'S GRACE WE STOOD UP!

In Matthew 24, our LORD Jesus answered three questions for the disciples. Their first question was about the Beautiful Temple, which Jesus told them would be destroyed with terrible calamity. This occurred in A.D. 70.

The other two questions were about the sign of His return and the end of the Age. Jesus told them of great tribulation at that time... which we have experienced worldwide.

20 *"**What shall be the sign of Your coming, and of the end of the age?**" (Ages last ~2,000 years; Jesus's advent started the Age of Pisces.)*

21*"For then shall be **great tribulation**, such as was not since the beginning of the world to this time, no, nor ever shall be.*

22 *And except those days should be shortened, there should no flesh be saved: but for the elect's sake those days shall be shortened."*

Thankfully, these days of tribulation are being shortened by the Great Awakening and the dismantling of the NWO Beast and False Prophet!

23 *"Then if any man shall say to you, Lo, here is Christ, or there; believe it not.*

24 *For there shall arise false Christs, and false prophets, and shall show great signs and wonders; insomuch that, if it were possible, they shall deceive the very elect.*

25 *Behold, I have told you before.*

26 *Wherefore if they shall say unto you, Behold, he is in the desert; go*

not forth: behold, he is in the secret chambers; believe it not.

27 For as the lightning comes out of the east, and shines even unto the west; so shall also the coming of the Son of Man be. **(this would be very obvious to everyone on earth)**

28 For wheresoever the carcass is, there will the eagles be gathered together. **(look for judgment falling on the cabal, and eagle warriors gathered to fight them – a sure sign)**

29 Immediately after the tribulation of those days shall the sun be darkened **(chemtrails)**, *and the moon shall not give her light* **(blood moons)**, *and the stars shall fall from heaven,* **(famous exposed)** *and the powers of the heavens shall be shaken* **(NWO/Beast's power broken)**:

*30 And then **shall appear the Sign of the Son of Man in heaven**,* **(Revelation 12 star sign 9/23/2017)** *and then shall all the tribes of the earth mourn, and they shall see the Son of Man coming in the* **clouds** *of heaven with power and great glory."* **(Some on earth are mourning the loss of their power. Some on earth are mourning as we struggle in this ferocious battle. The "clouds" symbolize Christ coming in great POWER, not physical clouds.)**

*31 And he shall send his angels with a great sound of a **trumpet**, and they shall gather together his elect from the four winds, from one end of heaven to the other.* **(Great Awakening and Patriots gathered worldwide)**

32 Now learn a parable of the fig tree; When his branch is yet tender, and puts forth leaves, you know that summer is nigh:

33 So likewise you, when you shall see all these things, know that it is near, even at the doors. **(Imminent Worldwide Liberation)**

34 Verily I say unto you, This generation **(age of ~2,000 years)** *shall not pass, till all these things be fulfilled."* (Matthew 24)

The tribulation is our struggle against the dark forces of the Beast/NWO. Satan has come down in great wrath, knowing he has <u>very</u> <u>little</u> <u>time</u>. He is throwing everything he's got at us, as Revelation 12 talks about the dragon going to war with the woman who gave birth to the child (Christ's kingdom). This Final Battle is between the Dragon and the 144,000. The deceived hear the rumblings, but they aren't fighting in the battle because they don't even know who the Beast is! The enemy wants to keep them asleep!

Now, let's finish Revelation 7, and see how those who have been victorious under great tribulation will be rewarded!

> 15 "Therefore are they before the throne of God, and serve him day and night in his temple: and he that sits on the throne shall dwell among them.
>
> 16 They shall hunger no more, neither thirst any more; neither shall the sun light on them, nor any heat.
>
> 17 For the Lamb which is in the midst of the throne shall feed them, and shall lead them to living fountains of waters: and God shall wipe away all tears from their eyes."

What a beautiful future we have! No more struggle! No more suffering! No more tears! He will make sure we are filled and satisfied! He will dwell with us on earth.

Ahhhhhh.....

Sounds like a wonderful vacation!

Well-deserved after the battle we've been through!

But we can't take a rest quite yet.

We've got to defeat these creeps!

We already identified several players in this epic cast!

The **EVIL HORSEMEN** are the enemy's methods of destruction - Anti-Christ Deception/War/Deprivation/and Death.

The **144,000** are those Knights/Elite Forces/SEALs/warriors who were chosen to fight in this Battle of Good versus Evil called Armageddon.

And the **GREAT MULTITUDE** are those who have been victorious over evil, refusing to be traitors or participate in satanic rituals to harm the innocent.

Now it's time to wake up humanity!

What is better to use than a TRUMPET BLAST?!

CHAPTER 10
TRUMPET BLASTS

I n Revelation Chapters 8 and 9, we hear seven TRUMPet Blasts!

Any idea what TRUMPets represent in God's Word? You're going to love this!

- Joshua used TRUMPet blasts to bring the walls of Jericho down!

- Gideon used TRUMPet blasts to defeat a huge army with 300 warriors!

- The Israelites used trumpets to call warriors to battle. But not like our trumpets. They used a shofar- which is a ram's horn.

Every year, at the beginning of the Harvest (in late September on the Gregorian calendar, the first of Tishrei on the Hebrew calendar), the Hebrews celebrate the Feast (or Festival) of

Trumpets. Actually they call it the Feast of Trump! How cool is that? The Feast of Trump is a **call to gather for repentance and restoration**! It begins with a loud trumpet blast! With that sound, the people are to gather together, and make up. This is their time to make right any wrongs. Restore anything that was taken. Restore relationships. Get completely right with their fellow man, and with the LORD. Then immediately after the Festival of Trumpets, they celebrate the Festival of Atonement, at which time all of their sins of the past year are forgiven. If they have not repented - returned what was stolen, restored broken relationships, made amends - then those sins are not forgiven. When Hebrews hear trumpets, they immediately think of the Feast of Trumpets.

Trumpets were also blown to announce the arrival of the King. And trumpet blasts were used to gather warriors for battle. When going into battle, their enemies would hear trumpets, and realize they were under attack! I LOVE that our President is named TRUMP. The prophetic implications of that name cannot be overstated. No doubt President Donald J. Trump is the anointed of the LORD for this Great Day of battle.

So what is the purpose of the seven trumpet blasts in Revelation Chapter 8? The trumpets signal warnings on those who are willfully following satan, and they are intended to stir them to TURN BACK before judgment falls! The trumpets are also intended to **WAKE UP** the people, so they can fight the Beast/ New World Order.

We have all experienced this awakening blast at some point. We were going along our normal routine. When something snapped us awake. For many of us, we heard that trumpet blast just before the 2016 election. Come to think of it, it was right around the Feast of Trumpets! I think the Feast of Trumpets was actually the **WAKE UP CALL** for The Great Awakening. More on that prophecy fulfillment at the end of this chapter.

When I heard something about the Wikileaks and the Weiner

laptop that had reduced hardened investigators to tears, I woke up with a jolt. And then as I dug, I discovered that the Bushes and the Clintons were not political rivals, but were in cahoots on the drug trafficking into Mena, Arkansas. After that, I was WIDE AWAKE!

Like someone had blasted a trumpet in my ears! I've been researching and fighting to expose these creeps ever since.

But many refuse to wake up, no matter what.

Some need to wake up and join the fight.

Others need to wake up and leave the New World Order.

Either way.... **WAKE UP!!**

The Seventh Seal—the Trumpet Call to Wake Up

Revelation 8

> 1 *"When the Lamb broke the seventh seal, there was silence in heaven for about half an hour.*
>
> 2 *And I saw the **seven angels** who stand before God, and **seven trumpets** were given to them.*
>
> 3 *Another angel came and stood at the altar, holding a golden censer; and much incense was given to him, so that he might add it to the prayers of all the saints on the golden altar which was before the throne.*
>
> 4 *And the smoke of the incense, with the prayers of the saints, went up before God out of the angel's hand.*
>
> 5 *Then the angel took the censer and filled it with the fire of the altar, and threw it to the earth; and there followed **peals of thunder and sounds and flashes of lightning and an earthquake.**"*

Woah. What an incredible vision John saw! Angels with trumpets ready to wake up humanity from their far too long winter's nap. You would think with all the peals of thunder and lightning flashes plus an earthquake, people would wake up. But some people sleep right through storms. As we have learned.

There was silence in heaven for half an hour. As if everyone in heaven had been busy doing their normal routine, as we had been, and then everyone stopped. They all knew the time to fight the beast had come. They knew it was going to be a rough ride. A real war. A war to end all wars. So they stopped and had a moment of silence. I think our loved ones prayed silently for us.

The more we have learned about what has been going on, literally beneath our feet, the more fervent our prayers have become for justice and righteousness to be established on the earth.

Notice the angel adds incense to our prayers, and the smoke of the incense and our prayers ascend to God. What could the incense represent? What is added to our prayers? Remember, the Holy Spirit groans for us in words that cannot be uttered. (Romans 8:26) We don't know how to pray as we ought. We don't see the complete picture. We don't have all the information. But the Holy Spirit does, and He perfects our prayers and they ascend to God. And God answers in the perfect, wisest, most effective way. Not one prayer is forgotten nor unanswered. We are filling those bowls that will bring judgment on the Beast/NWO.

This chapter will show terrible plagues on the earth. Many commentators interpret the plagues as God sending horrifying, indiscriminate devastation on all mankind. This is not a correct interpretation and has caused overwhelming and unnecessary fear.

SPECIAL NOTE: The angels blow the trumpets to **WAKE UP** the people to <u>WHO IS RESPONSIBLE</u> for the evil that is happening on earth. **THE ANGELS ARE <u>NOT</u> THE ONES INFLICTING DESTRUCTION ON HUMANITY.**

Make sure to keep that in mind as we go.

A single trumpet blast is enough to wake some people.

But watch the seven trumpets in this chapter.

They will get louder.

This first trumpet reveals a terrible storm.

How appropriate.

Our "favorite" knows the Bible.

> 6 "And the seven angels who had the seven trumpets prepared themselves to sound them. 7 The first sounded, and there came hail and fire, mixed with blood, and they were thrown to the earth."

This trumpet reveals a storm. And it's a doozy - Hail, Fire, and Blood.

We have learned that the New (Naaa-zi) World Order made terrifying advancements in their skill at manipulating the weather to cause storms during the Vietnam War. Search Ben Livingston, Weaponized Weather and HAARP. The NWO can produce storms, whip up hurricanes, cause floods, earthquakes, and tornadoes, even simulate lightning with their laser technology to take out entire neighborhoods. All before breakfast!

Yes, the NWO wielded their terrifying power. But when a hurricane hangs in the sky for 13 days straight, flooding a city as huge as Houston, or laser beams reduce houses to ash while nearby trees are left intact, that's a **WAKE UP CALL** from an angel!

What awakened us to realize we MUST destroy the Beast/NWO? I think we would all agree. The earth has been burning down around our ears! The suffering. The death. The wars. The cancer. The trafficking of children. The drug addiction. We have **all** suffered effects of their evil. When we realized this evil had been done INTENTIONALLY, that was our **WAKE UP CALL**.

They produced their evil storms, but now it's time for THE STORM. God's Storm. And His storm is not against humanity. His storm is against the evildoers. The criminal secret society cabal. The first five trumpets are EXPOSING THEM! How do I know that?

1/3 = 33% = 33°

*7 "and a **third** of the earth was burned up, and a **third** of the trees were burned up, and all the green grass was burned up."*

Every time you read 1/3, think Masonic Secret Society Cabal. Just like 1/3 of the angels rebelled against God.

Now that you are awake, every time you look at poisoned soil and plants, what do you think? That the 33° Masonic secret society is responsible. Their tall <u>tree</u> leadership, their dark <u>earthy</u> underground satanic minions, and every one of them that covered the world like grass, and raked in a lot of <u>green</u> cash by being part of their evil agenda.

The New World Order has caused death and devastation worldwide - on great and small, believers and unbelievers. These plagues are a natural consequence of the evil they have intentionally inflicted, and finally the angels have blown the trumpets to let us know.

It is not necessary to know exactly what each symbol in Revelation represents.

It is only necessary to **WAKE UP**.... and **FIGHT.**

*8 "The second angel sounded, and something like a great mountain burning with fire was thrown into the sea; and a **third** of the sea became blood,*

*9 and a **third** of the creatures which were in the sea and had life, died; and a **third** of the ships were destroyed."*

I'm sure you already know this, but there won't be a literal burning mountain that is thrown into the sea. Or blood in 1/3 of the sea, or 1/3 of sea creatures dead, or 1/3 of ships destroyed. So what could these symbolize?

This mountain surely represents the New World Order pyramid burning down. Remember the day you discovered what that strange pyramid on your (fake) dollar bill was for? Remember we were told how their evil scheme worked? The worldwide organizational structure. The players. The bloodlines. The puppet leaders.   The central banks. The media's role. Yeah. That is a loud trumpet **WAKE UP CALL.** (Maybe he is an angel, after all. :))

The sea usually represents humanity, so likely the "sea becoming blood" represents the devastation they have caused on our health and safety. Just look at the countless cancer centers worldwide and there's your **WAKEUP CALL**. Likely the "1/3 sea life died" represents the damage to the health of animals and birds and fish, intentionally caused by the New World Order. Just look at a chicken from the 50's and a chicken now, and there's your **WAKEUP CALL**!

The ships represent commerce and financial security. Of course, the financial crisis and the joblessness due to their hoarding of capital, and their monopoly on business, profiting on slave labor, has been another **HUGE WAKEUP CALL!**

Every time you see 1/3, the angels are pointing their fingers squarely at the New World Order satanists.

33°

You did it, New World Order! And you will pay!

Ready for the third trumpet?

> 10 "The third angel sounded, and a great star fell from heaven, burning like a torch, and it fell on a **third** of the rivers and on the springs of waters.

> 11 The name of the star is called Wormwood; and a **third** of the waters became wormwood, and many men died from the waters, because they were made bitter."

I believe Wormwood is exactly what is says. Toxins. Poisons causing diseases like cancer, and clinical depression, seizures, dizziness, migraines, Alzheimer's, and more diseases than I can name here. The burning torch reminds us of something causing smoke in the sky. Hmmm... what could that be? This has got to be symbolic of the toxic chem-metal trails. They've poisoned the water too. It keeps their hospitals full. And the cemeteries full. And their bank accounts full. It is looking like the CDC and WHO are the ones who perpetrate this horrific crime. Wormwood.

Don't you feel like shouting, "Could everybody please look up at the sky and **WAKE UP?!**"

Again with 1/3.

Yep. We are holding you responsible, you evil Masonic secret societies that used your secret oaths to take over and destroy the world.

We see you now.

1/3. 33° Got it. NWO. Baal-worshipers. Satanists.

> 12 "The fourth angel sounded, and a **third** of the sun and a **third** of the moon and a **third** of the stars were struck, so that a **third** of them would be darkened and the day would not shine for a **third** of it, and the night in the same way."

No doubt this is another devastating effect of the chem-metal trails (geoengineeringwatch.org). We can't see the sun or the moon or the stars! Losing a third of the sunlight affects our physical and mental health. I can personally attest to pea-soup skies giving me a bad attitude. And the plants don't like it either. (Unless they are genetically-modified crops by Bill Gates and his band of evil naaaa-zi scientists.)

Their concoction of Barium (BA) and Aluminum (AL), (and more), that we breathe 24/7 kept us from waking up to their crimes for a long time, and even made us a living antenna for more of their evil schemes. I wish I was kidding.

Day and night. They won't stop spraying.

You did notice the 1/3, right?

1/3 of the sun.   33° - It's your fault, NWO!

1/3 of the moon.   33° - It's your fault, NWO!

1/3 of the stars.   33° - It's your fault, NWO!

Pay us back for all the sunlight we have missed.

Pay us back for all the moonlight we have missed.

Pay us back for all the starlight we have missed.

And, in the next few chapters, you will discover why the NWO did NOT want us to be able to see the moon and stars. It's because God put them there for signs for us. The NWO knows these signs. But the "elite" hid these amazing signs from our view.

SHOUT "Look in the sky, normies. **WAKE .... UP!!!!**"

The more I write, the madder I get.

> 13 *"Then I looked, and I heard an eagle flying in midheaven, saying with a loud voice, "Woe, woe, woe to those who dwell on the earth, because of the remaining blasts of the trumpet of the three angels who are about to sound!"*

I think the eagle is mad too.

WOE to these creeps. And WOE to us all, because they are not going down without a fight.

They were invisible for so long. But no more.

So, the eagle is warning us too, that the storm is going to get fiercer with these last three trumpet blasts.

Because the enemy knows many of us are awake and they can't stop us. But the normies are still sound asleep. The NWO sleeping potion is strong!

GEEEEEZ!

... continuing with Revelation Chapter 9

> 1 *"And the fifth angel sounded, and I saw a star fall from heaven unto the earth: and to him was given the key of the bottomless pit.*
>
> 2 *And he opened the bottomless pit; and there arose a smoke out of the pit, as the smoke of a great furnace; and the sun and the air were darkened by reason of the smoke of the pit.*
>
> 3 *And there came out of the smoke locusts upon the earth: and unto them was given power, as the scorpions of the earth have power.*

Remember, we are not fighting flesh and blood. The fifth angel is warning us that the enemy will hit us with everything he's got, covering the earth like locust demons straight from the pits of hell.

4 "And it was commanded them that they should not hurt the grass of the earth, neither any green thing, neither any tree; but only those men which have not the seal of God in their foreheads."

But, they are not allowed to touch us. These lying locusts can only frighten and confuse. More on that in a minute.

What about this seal of God? Remember how I told you the warriors are sealed - knighted - ordained - for battle?

We heard the call to battle.

We know the enemy is the New World Order.

We know the battle plans.

We trust the plan.

We know the fake news works for them.

We are not easily fooled by their fake news or tricks.

But the normies?

They are confused and scared and deceived.

They keep listening to and believing the lies.

Paralyzed as with a scorpion sting.

Tricky deception that is no doubt from the pits of hell. Even yes, sorcery. Oppression. Coordinated by the Mainstream Media (MSM), the enemy of the people. Fostered by Hollywood and false teachers of every type.

STOP LISTENING TO THEM! And you will **WAKE UP!**

Their stings of deception are intended to frighten and confuse and control, but they have actually caused people to dig for truth. To ask God to guide them to the right answers. That's what we have done. And the LORD continually answers. Thank You LORD!

*5 "And to them it was given that they should not kill them, but that they should be tormented **five months**: and their torment was as the torment of a scorpion, when he strikes a man.*

6 And in those days shall men seek death, and shall not find it; and shall desire to die, and death shall flee from them.

7 And the shapes of the locusts were like unto horses prepared unto battle; and on their heads were as it were crowns like gold, and their faces were as the faces of men.

8 And they had hair as the hair of women, and their teeth were as the teeth of lions.

9 And they had breastplates, as it were breastplates of iron; and the sound of their wings was as the sound of chariots of many horses running to battle.

*10 And they had tails like unto scorpions, and there were stings in their tails: and their power was to hurt men **five months**.*

11 And they had a king over them, which is the angel of the bottomless pit, whose name in the Hebrew tongue is Abaddon, but in the Greek tongue has his name Apollyon."

How about this for a weird section of the Bible?

Locusts like horses with a man's face and woman's hair, and a scorpion's tail. The prophecy buffs have had fun with this one!

I think these locusts are FAKE NEWS!

It makes perfectly good sense after having seen the lengths these people will go to, in order to frighten the masses into submission. Yes, Fake News is Mainstream Media, but it is also "officials," "governors," "experts," "celebrities," even "Antifa-type groups," and "fake patriots" and "trolls" throughout the internet! The confusion and injustice can make people feel like giving up on life entirely. Add that to the effects of GMOs on our hormones... and the depression and suicidal thoughts are REAL! Thankfully, most do not follow through on these horrible impulses. At the time I am writing this update, we are right in the middle of the Covid19 worldwide pandemic. President Trump warned that quarantining and job loss could lead to suicide, so he wants to open the economy as quickly as possible.

These demonic locusts from the bottomless pit, masquerading as "experts," amuse themselves by toying with normies. It's like an evil game of cat and mouse.   Literally there is no bottom to the pit of lies they will go to in their deception. They profess to be trustworthy, and then strike the unsuspecting viewers from behind.   These are the stings in their tails. They agitate. They strike fear. They paralyze, depress, and confuse. Ultimately to control the masses.   Once you are awake, you realize they are experts in deception.   Truly the enemy of the people, the "hidden enemy," as President Trump has told us.

They lead the masses to believe, "The world is a scary place. This is how it will always be, normies, so there is no reason to fight it. We will take care of you, and tell you what to believe." It's like reruns of the movie "1984" looping in the background! Maddening. "You're getting sleepy," in their hypnotic trance.

With their fancy broadcast studios, and their pretty faces and their salon-perfect hair, they authoritatively wear their golden crowns to order the masses of sheep wherever they want them to go.   Did you notice this passage said they have the faces of men, but the hair of women? How many times have you looked at an "expert official" and wondered, "Is that a man made to look like a woman?   Or vice versa?" They are trying to make our minds normalize to their perversion, just as God told us they would in this Revelation Chapter 9.

And what of their lions' teeth and breastplates?   They don't just tell little white lies. Their lies are like a lion ripping apart our society, our economy, our families, our ability to reason, and our faith.   It's as if they have breastplates over their hearts. Completely unfeeling and heartless to the devastating effects of their lies.

And what about the frightening sound of "chariots with many horses running to battle?"   That might remind you of Second Kings 7, where they heard sounds they thought were chariots approaching, so they ran away when no one was even pursuing them. THAT is a perfect example of the mainstream fear-mongering media. They scare people to death over NOTHING!

With their scary made-up news stories.... War here! Disease there! Storms here! Devastation there! BLLLLAAAAHHH!! Who needs a haunted house when you have the MSM?

Of course, they've been doing this forever.

They never let a good lie go to waste! Where do all these lies come from? The Mainstream Media,

is fed by Reuters and the Associated Press,

which is fed by the evil bloodline banksters,

which is fed by Abaddon - the Destroyer - himself.

So, when you are watching these "MSM official experts," you are watching Abaddon News!

So **WAKE UP! TURN IT OFF!**

******* I am so thankful President Trump helped us to see through their lies. *******

The NWO is trying desperately to stop President Trump, the Great Awakening, and the judgment for their crimes against humanity.

The enemy is trying to keep the masses asleep. But their over-the-top tricks are actually a very loud trumpet blast that is **WAKING UP** the masses.

How are these **WAKE UP CALLS** affecting the sheeple? It is boomeranging! The enemy went too far. By trying to stop us, they awakened the normies! Because fear drives people to get answers. Fear drives people to the truth. The LORD always has a good reason for allowing the enemy any latitude with his sheep. And it is always meant for good. To draw them. To make them aware of what they maybe have denied… that they need to run to His side fast!

I think this **WAKE UP CALL** is also intended for some of the low-level minions of the secret society. They might have wanted to get rich and powerful, but they don't want to be a part of causing a worldwide pandemic!

> *"The LORD is not willing that any should perish, but that all should come to repentance."* (2nd Peter 3:9)

The LORD is so patient and kind to send these **WAKE UP CALLS**.

NOW, on to the sixth trumpet!

THE TABLES HAVE TURNED!

> *12 "One woe is past; and, behold, there come two woes more hereafter.*
>
> *13 And the sixth angel sounded, and I heard a voice from the four horns of the golden altar which is before God,*
>
> *14 Saying to the sixth angel which had the trumpet, "Loose the four angels which are bound in the great river Euphrates"."*

Two more Woes.

TERRORS.

What is coming will be <u>shocking</u> to the world.

But it will be TERRIFYING to the New World Order. We know there are currently ~170,000 sealed federal indictments. Imagine the rich and powerful being arrested and convicted of their crimes against humanity. Imagine their fall from power and wealth and prestige to Gitmo with "a pot and a cot," and becoming the despised of the earth. WOE.

So this angel blasts its trumpet from the **horns** of the altar. What is the significance of the horns? It's pretty cool, actually. If someone was in danger and needed safety or asylum, they could put their hands on the horns of the altar, and they would be safe. The horns are like "home base" in a game of tag.

At one point in the book of Amos, the horns were broken off, symbolizing there was <u>no safe zone</u>. Boy, isn't that the truth?! But, by a miracle, with the blast of the sixth trumpet, the horns are back! There is a voice coming from the horns! "Safety and justice are back!"

Remember my SPECIAL NOTE earlier in this chapter?

The angels blow the trumpets to **WAKE UP** the people to <u>WHO IS RESPONSIBLE</u> for the evil that is happening on earth. **THE ANGELS ARE NOT THE ONES INFLICTING DESTRUCTION ON HUMANITY.**

But now, finally, it is time to

LOOSE THE ANGELS OF GOD!

14 "Saying to the sixth angel which had the trumpet, "Loose the four angels which are bound in the great river Euphrates"."

How do I know these are God's Angels? Just look at the last verse of Chapter 9. These angels are going after the satan-worshipers to destroy them! Finally!!

So let's break down these verses. You know where the Euphrates is, right? That is where the Garden of Eden was. The birthplace of humanity. The place, symbolically speaking, that we all long for, but these four angels are keeping us out. Why? Because it is the place of Original Sin and the Fall of Man and the Tree of Life. Because the LORD does not want us to live in a sinful, rebellious condition forever. He wants peace on earth, good will toward man, not hell on earth forever. It has taken 6,000 years, and we are finally ready to kick the Beast out of this earth! That is humanity's first step back to Eden.

15 "And the four angels were loosed, which were prepared for an hour, *and a day, and a month, and a year, for to slay the **third** part of men.*

16 And the number of the army of the horsemen were two hundred thousand thousand: and I heard the number of them."

These angels have been waiting 6,000 years to destroy these 33° creeps. There is an exact hour and day and month and year when they will do exactly that. And they will be joined by 200 Million horsemen. That's us!! If someone tells you that battle is on a typical battlefield, ask them to get medical attention. No doubt this battle is an information war with Patriots rising up all around the world, exposing the criminals and their crimes against humanity, wherever it is found. This is the Angels and Patriots who are fighting the New World Order Beast. This great army will SLAY 1/3 of them! What does 1/3 symbolize?

33%

33°

We will DESTROY THE NEW WORLD ORDER 33° SECRET SOCIETY!!!!

But you might ask, "I thought the number was 144,000. Why does this passage say 200 Million?

I think the 144,000 is a symbolic number representing the Armageddon warriors. But the 200 Million just might be pretty close to the actual number. John said he heard that <u>exact number</u>. 200 Million sounds like a LOT of people, and it is. But with 7.7 Billion people on earth, 200 Million comes to only ~2.5% of humanity. Sounds like Gideon's army, where the LORD used a small number of warriors so everyone would know the victory was the LORD'S! (see the FreedomForce.LIVE social media link for tons of videos from the Bible, including the story of Gideon.) What an honor to be in the Angel/Patriot Army of the LORD!!! It's so cool the LORD gave us all these Bible "codes" and is teaching us to read them!

17 "And I saw the horses in the vision, and them that sat on them, having breastplates of fire, and of jacinth, and brimstone: and the heads of the horses were as the heads of lions; and out of their mouths issued fire and smoke and brimstone."

The warriors have breastplates of fire and brimstone! That's us for sure! We have fire and brimstone in our hearts and we won't stop until this enemy receives the just penalty for their crimes! Our horses have heads like lions. Now that's one funny-looking horse! But what if our horses are our social media accounts on which we ride through the internet, roaring and devouring every evil?! Our Twitter and Facebook and YouTube accounts breathe out fire and brimstone on a daily basis! We are burning a hole in the MSM locusts' narrative and we are destroying them! That's what we Patriots have done ever since the first trumpet blast! WE DO NOT SLEEP!

*18 "By these three was the **third** part of men killed, by the fire, and by the smoke, and by the brimstone, which issued out of their mouths.*

*19 For their power is in their **mouth**, and in their **tails**: for their tails were like unto serpents, and had heads, and with them they do hurt."*

Fire and Smoke and Brimstone.

Remember at the beginning of Chapter 8, the angel threw down the fire from God's altar, mixed with the Holy smoke of the Holy Spirit, mixed with our prayers?

Fire is the Holy Judgment Fire from God's altar.

Smoke is the Holy Spirit of God Who empowers us.

Brimstone is vehement or condemnatory rhetoric, especially rhetoric warning of the torments of hell for immoral behavior. (from FreeDictionary.com) Yep that pretty much sums up our social media posts.

Our fiery, Holy Spirit-inspired condemning rhetoric is exposing their horrific crimes and crying out for arrests and prosecution! These are the three powerful weapons that come out of our mouths that we are using to destroy the 33°. These coals of justice burn within our hearts, and won't be extinguished until the last of these criminals is cast out of the earth.

Verse 19 says our power is also in our tails. I think that

symbolizes the power we have had to destroy the enemy by surprise. They never suspected that a band of rag-tag digital soldiers could destroy their evil empire! (Hahahahha- evil laugh)

But after everything we have done, many of them Still. Won't. Stop. Doesn't this verse sound just like these creeps we are fighting?

> 20 "And the rest of the men which were not killed by these plagues, yet repented not of the **works of their hands, that they should not worship devils**, and **idols of gold, and silver, and brass, and stone, and of wood**: which neither can see, nor hear, nor walk:
>
> 21 Neither repented they of their **murders**, nor of their **sorceries**, nor of their **fornication**, nor of their **thefts**."

These sins mentioned here are not your typical Class D misdemeanor. They do horrific crimes, even satanic ritual murders, and are unrepentant. This is not just a regular person with a bad attitude, or someone who occasionally slips up.

Many Bible teachers teach that every sin is the same.

NO IT IS NOT.

PLEASE. Eyeroll. SMH.

There is a HUGE difference between satanists' sins, and sins regular people commit.

"Think for yourself."

Remember the teaching about the "sin leading to death" or the "sin unto death," also called "the blasphemy of the Holy Spirit"? THAT means the satanic rituals and human sacrifice that these evildoers commit. Rituals and crimes straight from the pits of hell that are so evil, we are not even encouraged to pray for them!

> "If any man see his brother sin a sin which is not unto death, he shall ask, and he shall give him life for them that sin not unto death. There is a sin unto death: I do not say that he shall pray for it. All unrighteousness is sin: and there is a sin not unto death." (1st John 5:16-17)

In other words, these people have asked the demons to possess them, and they demanded the Holy Spirit leave.

> *"Wherefore I say unto you, all manner of sin and blasphemy shall be forgiven unto men: but the blasphemy against the Holy Ghost shall not be forgiven unto men."* (Matthew 12:31)

The New World Order is deceived - and happily so. They have hardened their hearts to a shocking degree. In this chapter we see that they refuse to turn back to God despite all the terrible consequences that come from a life of rebellion against God, and the certain terrifying judgment to come. They can't find the humility to turn back to God. Apostate. "Let them alone." (Matthew 15) Because they clearly REFUSE to repent, this is what the LORD MUST do:

> *"then shall that Wicked* (New World Order Beast) *be revealed, whom* **the Lord shall consume with the spirit of his mouth, and shall destroy with the brightness of his coming:**
>
> *9 Even him, whose coming is after the working of satan with all power and signs and lying wonders,* **(New World Order)**
>
> *10 And with all deceivableness of unrighteousness in them that perish; because they received not the love of the truth, that they might be saved.*
>
> *11* **And for this cause God shall send them strong delusion, that they should believe a lie:**
>
> *12* **That they all might be damned who believed not the truth, but had pleasure in unrighteousness."** (2nd Thess. 2:8-12)

The demon-worshipers STILL refuse to repent and turn back to God. They are under STRONG delusion. These criminals actually get pleasure out of unrighteousness. It is just as we have seen in this battle. The Deep State keeps doubling down on their crimes and deception. They continue to project their crimes onto others, especially on our Commander-in-Chief! They will pay.

How timely is the Book of Revelation?! It portrays exactly what we are seeing before our very eyes! When we look at these people, we wonder why they do this. Why they won't turn back.

93

They look so normal on the outside. But the darkness has eaten away their souls. Sick. It is a huge redpill. And John gets the first one.

CHAPTER 11
REDPILLED

I n Revelation Chapter 10, the Apostle John was red-pilled. The good news was that the world would be set free from the enemy! But when John learned what had been happening all around him, he became nauseous. We know exactly how he felt.

Revelation 10

1 "And I saw another mighty angel come down from heaven, clothed with a cloud: and a rainbow was upon his head, and his face was as it were the sun, and his feet as pillars of fire:

Check out this angel! Clothed with a cloud! A rainbow on his head! Face lit up like the sun! And feet like fire! That's one cool angel!

Remember, we have learned that the angels are represented by the wandering stars: Venus, Mercury, Jupiter, Mars, and Saturn. And they are sending us messages - signs the LORD put in the heavens for us! Like a heavenly code! So any idea which one this might be?

We have several clues. Which star is lit up by the sun? In other words, which one is closest to the sun? Which one has feet like fire because it moves so rapidly? Ask your third grader if you're a little light on astronomy. How about the FTD Florist logo? It's Mercury!

Mercury sparkles like a rainbow and loops around the sun in just 79 days like a whirlwind cloud. Beautiful!

The heavens declare the glory of God! So what is this messenger declaring?

ONLY THE GREAT AWAKENING OF HUMANITY!

Check out Mercury looping in Aquarius starting in January 2020! This is the Dawning of the Age of Aquarius for sure! Mercury says so! Aquarius symbolizes the LORD pouring His Spirit on all flesh... and that is what is happening on earth!

So what has Mercury got to say? He's loaded with redpills for normies! And that's the "Mass Start Awakening" we've been waiting for! This Covid Plandemic has shaken humanity awake! What? Someone planned this %$@&! They tried to kill off humanity and destroy our economy! So they could stop Trump? Lemme at em!

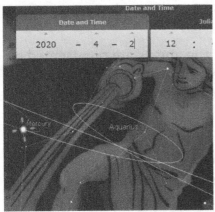

Revelation 10

*1 "And I saw another mighty angel come down from heaven, **clothed with a cloud: and a rainbow was upon his head, and his face was as it were the sun, and his feet as pillars of fire:***

2 And he had in his hand a little book open: and he set his right foot upon the sea, and his left foot on the earth,

3 And cried with a loud voice, as when a lion roars: and when he had cried, seven thunders uttered their voices.

4 And when the seven thunders had uttered their voices, I was about to write: and I heard a voice from heaven saying unto me, Seal up those things which the seven thunders uttered, and write them not.

5 And the angel which I saw stand upon the sea and upon the earth lifted up his hand to heaven,

6 And the angel swore by him that lives for ever and ever, who created heaven, and the things that therein are, and the earth, and the things that therein are, and the sea, and the things which are therein, that there should be time no longer:

7 But in the days of the voice of the seventh angel, when he shall begin to sound, the mystery of God should be finished, as he has declared to his servants the prophets.

8 And the voice which I heard from heaven spoke to me again, and said, Go and take the little book which is open in the hand of the angel which stands upon the sea and upon the earth.

9 And I went to the angel, and said to him, Give me the little book. And he said to me, Take it, and eat it; and it shall make your belly bitter, but it shall be in your mouth sweet as honey.

10 And I took the little book out of the angel's hand, and ate it up; and it was in my mouth sweet as honey: and as soon as I had eaten it, my belly was bitter.

11 And he said unto me, You must prophesy again before many peoples, and nations, and tongues, and kings."

True prophets have Good News to share, but they also MUST tell the truth about those who do wickedness! Mercury is standing on the sea <u>and</u> on the land. So he is going to reveal to the world how they were enslaved by the "Law of the Seas"/Admiralty Law, and how the "Law of the Land" minions did the Beast's dirty work! He is going to tell the truth about satan-worshipers and the "sick" things they do. About their vile, wicked rituals from the pits of hell. Of how they take pleasure in wickedness, even glee at the misery, despair, and pain they intentionally inflict. True prophets are compelled to tell of the lies and corruption, to warn the people of the evil plots of the CDC and the Federal Reserve and more. Even though it churns their stomachs.

Buckle up! Because once humanity gets nauseous, it will be time to cast these despicable creeps into the abyss!

CHAPTER 12
WITNESSES

Revelation 11 is one of my favorite parts of the book of Revelation. At first, it might seem like the most impossible chapter to understand. So much symbolism! But once you have the keys – which I will share with you – you will love it too!

First off, here John goes again. He's going to tell about the turmoil, but he is compelled to tell how it will culminate in the glorious Kingdom where Christ will reign on earth. It's as if John can't tell the story without telling the good part... the absolutely sure victory that is coming. Thanks John, because so many people seem to drone on and on and on about the bad news, and leave no time for the good news! So first, read through the passage, and I will break it down for you.

Revelation 11

1 "And there was given me a reed like unto a rod: and the angel stood, saying, Rise, and measure the temple of God, and the altar, and them that worship therein.

2 But the court which is without the temple leave out, and measure it not; for it is given unto the Gentiles: and the holy city shall they tread under foot forty and two months.

*3 And I will give power unto my two witnesses, and they shall prophesy a **thousand two hundred and threescore days**, clothed in sackcloth.*

4 These are the two olive trees, and the two candlesticks standing before the God of the earth.

5 And if any man will hurt them, fire proceeds out of their mouth, and devours their enemies: and if any man will hurt them, he must in this manner be killed.

6 These have power to shut heaven, that it rain not in the days of their prophecy: and have power over waters to turn them to blood, and to smite the earth with all plagues, as often as they will.

7 And when they shall have finished their testimony, the beast that ascends out of the bottomless pit shall make war against them, and shall overcome them, and kill them.

8 And their dead bodies shall lie in the street of the great city, which spiritually is called Sodom and Egypt, where also our Lord was crucified.

9 And they of the people and kindreds and tongues and nations shall see their dead bodies **three days and a half**, and shall not suffer their dead bodies to be put in graves.

10 And they that dwell upon the earth shall rejoice over them, and make merry, and shall send gifts one to another; because these two prophets tormented them that dwelt on the earth.

11 And after **three days and a half the spirit of life from God entered into them, and they stood upon their feet**; and great fear fell upon them which saw them.

12 And they heard a great voice from heaven saying unto them, Come up hither. And they **ascended up to heaven in a cloud**; and their enemies beheld them.

13 And the same hour was there a great earthquake, and the tenth part of the city fell, and in the earthquake were slain of men seven thousand: and the remnant were frightened, and gave glory to the God of heaven.

14 The second woe is past; and, behold, the third woe comes quickly.

15 And the seventh angel sounded; and there were great voices in heaven, saying, The kingdoms of this world are become the kingdoms of our Lord, and of his Christ; and he shall reign for ever and ever.

16 And the four and twenty elders, which sat before God on their seats, fell upon their faces, and worshiped God,

17 Saying, We give thee thanks, O Lord God Almighty, which art, and wast, and art to come; because you have taken to yourself your great power, and have begun to reign.

18 And the nations were angry, and your wrath is come, and the time of the dead, that they should be judged, and that you should give reward unto your servants the prophets, and to the saints, and them that fear your name, small and great; and should destroy them which destroy the earth.

19 And the temple of God was opened in heaven, and there was seen in his temple the ark of his testament: and there were lightnings, and voices, and thunderings, and an earthquake, and great hail."

So I'm guessing you see what I mean by all the strange symbolism in this chapter! It took some doing, a lifetime of Bible study, and asking the LORD for understanding, but now I'm absolutely convinced I have the keys to unlock this chapter. Here goes!

> 1 *"And there was given me a reed like a rod: and the angel stood, saying, Rise, and measure the temple of God, and the altar, and them that worship therein."*

At first, John measured/examined/judged the Church. As we know, "Judgment begins in the house of God."

What condition is the Church in?

Are believers solid in Biblical understanding?

Are they strong in their relationship with the LORD to walk in His ways with their whole hearts?

Are they using their time and talents for His Kingdom, and to reach those who are outside the family of God?

He measured the altar as if to determine their true devotion to Christ.

Are they walking in purity and love?

Do they love their neighbors as themselves?

Do they draw close to Christ so they aren't entangled with the love of money and accolades?

Do they have a strong sense of justice, and the fortitude to fight for it?

John doesn't give us the measurements here, but we do know from other places in Scripture, that at the end of the age, there will be a famine of hearing the Word of the LORD (Amos 8:11), and there will be so much deception, that the question is asked,

"When the Lord returns will He find faith on the earth?" (Luke 18:8)

The fact is, that in order to fight the Great Battle of Armageddon, we need people of God to measure up.

They absolutely MUST have a strong sense of justice and honor, nerves of steel, with their trust firmly in the LORD, and a close relationship with Him to hear where He directs them. Those are the ones who get to ride with the LORD into the fierce battle.

> 2 "But the court which is outside the temple leave out, and measure it not; for it is given to the Gentiles: and the holy city shall they tread under foot forty and two months."

Why do the Gentiles (evildoers) trample on the holy city (God's people) for 42 months? Because that's what evildoers do. They trample. Since they are not walking in a right relationship with God, and operating under the power of the Holy Spirit, they trample. They trample rights and laws. They trample feelings. They trample sensibilities. They don't think it strange at all to have a society without God, because they live their entire lives without God. And the more tramplers, the lower the society sinks.

> "Because the carnal mind is enmity against God; for **it is not subject to the law of God, nor indeed can be**." (Romans 8)

What about the 42 months? Well, from my research check out what I discovered.

42 months = 1,260 days = 3.5 years =
Time, Times and Half a Time.

Cool, huh? These are all equivalent and are used interchangeably in Daniel and Revelation. They always seem to indicate a long struggle between good and evil.

Here are two verses in Daniel:

Daniel 7:25
> "He shall speak great words against the Most High, and shall wear out the saints of the Most High, and think to change times and laws -- and they shall be **given into his hands until a time and times and the dividing of a time**."

Daniel 12:7
> "It shall be for a **time, times, and half a time** that he can scatter the power of the holy people."

So in this instance, the Gentiles (general term for evildoers) have trampled the holy people for far too long. Like when we say "time and again." It is symbolic language, not a calendar of specific time. That's not the answer Daniel wanted to hear. He was told, "But you, go on to the end and rest, and you will arise for your allotted inheritance at the end of the days." In other words, don't worry. Trust the Plan.

There has been so much trampling, for so long, but that's all <u>finally</u> starting to change!

Here's one more interesting find before we jump into the Great Awakening chapter!

The period of **42 weeks** is the length of time for Jupiter to complete a loop or a path in the heavens (see Chapter 13), and Jupiter represents Christ as the God of War. So the "42 weeks" seems to confirm the **42 months** symbolism, of a period of struggle/war.

> 3 *"And I will give power unto my two witnesses, and they shall prophesy **a thousand two hundred and threescore days**, clothed in sackcloth."* (Revelation 11)

Again with the 1,260 days/42 months symbolism. Again with the struggle. The witnesses testifying against the evildoers are in sackcloth, which symbolizes they are mourning over the evil that Just. Won't. Stop.

Let's look at the two witnesses. They aren't just any witnesses. They PROPHESY from the LORD. They speak and act on His behalf.

Think with me.

There is no way these two witnesses are individuals.

These two witnesses have to be symbolic.

I know. I know. The seminary professors say these two are individuals.

Hog.

Wash.

Remember how we talked about all the symbolism in Revelation?

This chapter is chock-full of symbolism!

So let's think.

What two "witnesses" has the LORD set up on earth?

They speak and act on His behalf.

They are mourning.

It's actually pretty easy when you think logically.

What group "prophesies"?

One of the witnesses is **Religious Institutions**, of course!

They keep society in check.

They help to keep society from breaking down into anarchy.

Maybe they have not accomplished their goal, especially in recent years, but their *intended* purpose is to motivate people to treat each other fairly... to help the defenseless... to follow God from the heart, and to make for an enjoyable and free society.

I will use the term *Religious Institutions*, because most of the world religions - Christianity, Judaism, Islam, Hinduism, and even Buddhism - were originally based on Abraham's faith in God. Sadly, they have all been infiltrated and hijacked, to one extent or another.

Ok, we got one of the witnesses figured out. As we move forward, you will agree, this is no doubt the correct interpretation.

What about the other witness?

What other institution maintains peace on earth?

Think Peace Officer.

Think Law and Order.

Think Barney Fife.

You got it!

The Government!!!

With what we know about the "Injustice System," you are probably rolling your eyes right now. But we are talking about the *intended* purpose for government.

Here's a very interesting passage about God's intention for government.

> *"Let every soul be subject to the governing authorities. For there is no authority except from God, and* **the authorities that exist are appointed by God.** *2 Therefore whoever resists the authority resists the ordinance of God, and those who resist will bring judgment on themselves. 3 For rulers are not a terror to good works, but to evil. Do you want to be unafraid of the authority? Do what is good, and you will have praise from the same. 4 For he is God's minister to you for good. But if you do evil, be afraid; for he does not bear the sword in vain;* **for he is God's minister, an avenger to execute wrath on him who practices evil."** (Romans 13)

The Government has authority to punish evildoers... from fines to prison to even worse. That is how they keep peace on the earth. Whether or not they have fulfilled that purpose is another matter. For the most part, the government is effective in keeping "the little people" from doing evil, for fear of punishment.

No doubt, the Government is the second witness!

Good Job!!

Ok, so we've gotten that far.

The two witnesses are the Religious Institutions and the Government. What do these two witnesses do? Witnesses testify to the truth. The Religious Institutions and the Government are supposed to testify to the truth, creating and maintaining a peaceful society.

How long do they do that? 1,260 days. That is the same period of time as the 42 months the Gentiles do their trampling. As long as there is evil, the Religious Institutions and the Government have a big job to do stamping it out! Even though I roll my eyes as I write that, just imagine our society WITHOUT Religious Institutions and Government.

It would be complete ANARCHY!

Isn't this making sense now?

(Reminds me of High School Language Arts class.)

Let's keep decoding the strange symbolism.

> 4 *"These are the two olive trees, and the two candlesticks standing before the God of the earth."*

Olive Trees are for healing.

Candlesticks give light.

Of course, candlesticks produce light which dispels darkness/ evil. So the Religious Institutions and the Government are supposed to shine His light to stop evil in this dark world. Jesus is the Light of the world and He promised that those who walk with Him will not walk in darkness... (evil). He even tells us we are the light of the world too... reflecting His light as we are led by His Spirit. That light brings truth and unity and justice...

> *"If we walk in the light as He is in the light, we have fellowship with one another. And the blood of Jesus Christ, His Son, cleanses us from all sin."* (1st John 1:7)

> *"And we have no fellowship with the unfruitful deeds of darkness, but we rather expose them."* (Ephesians 5:11)

Imagine if the Religious Institutions and Government were flooded with God's light! That would transform societies!

So what might the olive trees represent? Olive trees produce olive oil which is terrific for our health and healing! So the Religious Institutions and Government are intended to bring justice and freedom for the health and healing of our societies. Clean water, clean air, safe food, life, liberty, and the pursuit of happiness. No doubt this is the correct interpretation of the two witnesses!

> 5 *"And if any man will hurt them, fire proceeds out of their mouth, and devours their enemies: and if any man will hurt them, he must in this*

manner be killed."

In other words, "Don't break the law or you will be sorry!" Religious Institutions are supposed to speak God's Word so clearly that everyone knows the judgment of God for sin, and therefore lives a righteous life. And the Government has power to ENFORCE law and order, under penalty of serious punishment, so we can all live in peace.

This is getting easy! But the next one is going to require a little more Bible knowledge. Ready?

> 6 *"These have* **power to shut heaven, that it rain not in the days of their prophecy:** *and* **have power over waters to turn them to blood, and to smite the earth with all plagues,** *as often as they will."*

How about verse six? Any ideas? Who had *"power to shut heaven, that it rain not in the days of their prophecy"*?Remember Elijah? He courageously went up against Ahab and Jezebel about their Baal worship and child sacrifice rituals. In order to ENFORCE their compliance, Elijah prayed, and the rain stopped for 3.5 years! Now THAT got their attention! Imagine 3.5 years with NO RAIN! (Interesting that this witness directs our attention to the sins of the New World Order of Baal worship.) Elijah represents the Religious Institutions that are intended to pray and have similar power from the LORD to bring justice on the earth.

(* Who noticed the symbolism of 3.5 years of Elijah's struggle against Ahab and Jezebel? It's EVERYWHERE throughout the Word of God!)

Next, who had "power to turn the rivers to blood and to smite the earth with all plagues," as in verse six? You guessed it! It was Moses! No doubt the one who turned the rivers to blood was Moses. Moses represents the law (or government). These plagues finally got the attention of the evil, murdering task-master, Pharaoh. And the plagues were God's instrument to set the people free from Pharaoh's tyranny! (You know, this reminds me of the New World Order task-masters too!)

So in this chapter, Elijah represents the Religious Authority, and Moses represents Civil Government Authority... the two authorities on earth that are to maintain peace and justice. But... as the story goes, they are silenced. It doesn't say why. They just finish their testimony. Both stopped witnessing about the truth. Sound familiar?

For various reasons, both have been silenced and ineffective. We could blame it on prayer being taken out of schools, and on the utter onslaught against religion from all directions. We could blame it on the masonic influence that has crept in unawares into churches and other religious groups and seminaries. We could blame it on the busyness of our lives that has pushed out time to be in the Word of God. We could blame it on the filth we are force-fed if we ever turn on our televisions or movies or social media.

And the Government... oh don't get me started on that. From corrupt officials who run drug and human trafficking rings, to hijacked voting machines, to New World Order control of puppet candidates, to the utter takeover of our courts, and our Federal Reserve, and on and on. As Ronald Reagan said, "the Government IS the problem!"

> 7 "And when they shall have finished their testimony, the beast that ascends out of the bottomless pit shall make war against them, and shall overcome them, and kill them."

For whatever reason, the two witnesses – the Government and the Religious Institutions - were silenced. Incapable of doing their jobs of bringing light and healing to society. Most churches made a pact with the government not to speak about politics, and were given 501C3 tax exempt status, equating to 30 pieces of silver. The Johnson Amendment went a long way in silencing the churches in America.

How did John, 2,000 years ago, know this would happen?

God knew.

He knew the Beast would gain more and more and more power,

and take completely over.

But that's not all. The Beast isn't content for them to be silenced. The Beast kills them.

Dead.

Ineffective.

Not even alive to care.

Zombified.

Wiped out.

Isn't that what we have seen all over the earth? Religious buildings and Government buildings up and down every street, but the lawlessness took over. As hard as we have tried, we have been helpless to stop it. And the enemy has laughed. And laughed. And laughed.

The next verse is so weird, and I have even heard that this verse is literal. Come on now people! This is a symbolic passage if there ever was one. Can you figure it out?

> 8 "And their dead bodies shall lie in the street of the great city, which spiritually is called **Sodom and Egypt**, where also our Lord was crucified.
>
> 9 And they of the people and kindred and tongues and nations shall see their dead bodies **three days and a half**, and shall not suffer their dead bodies to be put in graves.
>
> 10 And they that dwell upon the earth shall rejoice over them, and make merry, and shall send gifts one to another; because these two prophets tormented them that dwelt on the earth."

Their bodies are dead. Lying in the street. What? That's crazy!! Just as crazy as when we drive all around our Country, and we see religious buildings and government buildings up and down every street, while at the same time we see pornography, and drug addiction, and corruption of every kind, and human trafficking, and broken families, and poverty, and godless entertainment everywhere. We've grown so accustomed to the evil, most of us aren't even shocked anymore. Most of us don't do much more about it than a dead body would.

And get this!

It says in the passage that they don't bury them!

(If you hear someone explaining that verse literally, please tell them to stop it.)

The point is, the New World Order Beast system doesn't want to tear down Religion and Government. No, No! That would awaken the masses. It is much more effective to leave them rotting in place, but stone-cold ineffective at restoring society. Demoralizing and Hopeless.

(* Who noticed the 3.5 days symbolism of the dead bodies in the street? See what I mean?)

So what's the point of them lying in Egypt and Sodom? Do you remember the predominant sins of these two? Egypt's predominant sins were tyranny and satan-worship. They enslaved God's people, causing them to suffer and starve and be killed. They committed abominable satanic rituals. What about Sodom? Their predominant sin was debauchery – sexual deviancy and an utter disregard for justice. So back to imagery lesson from High School language arts.... The Religious Institutions and the Government have been overcome by tyranny, satanic rituals, sexual deviancy, and an utter disregard for justice.

Any questions?

For those who are awake...

I think you know this is EXACTLY the perfect interpretation.

And to add insult to injury, look at what they do!

> "And they that dwell upon the earth shall rejoice over them, and make merry, and shall send gifts one to another; because these two prophets tormented them that dwelt on the earth."

The New World Order and their minions have laughed and laughed and laughed! Because they stopped the ones who were supposed to stop their evil!

They partied like it was 1999!

As they plotted the final enslavement of the masses.

Have I painted a hopeless enough picture for you?

"The ones who were intended to save society, are dead!"

Hopeless.

But...

Something happens.

It is my favorite verse in all of Revelation!

Maybe even in the entire Bible!

And it is verse 11:11!

HAHAHAHA!!!

You will know how great that is!

Ready?

You're going to love verse 11:11!

> "And after three days and a half **the spirit of life from God entered into them, and they stood upon their feet**; and great fear fell upon them which saw them."

The Spirit of Life from God entered us!!

And...

WE STOOD UP!!!!!!!

We stood up in America – and elected our wonderful President Donald J. Trump!

We stood up in Europe – with the Yellow Vest Movements, and elected strong leaders in Hungary and Poland and Italy – throwing off Soros and the EU!

We stood up in Brazil, and now in Venezuela!

We stood up even in Saudi Arabia - the head of evil human trafficking!

We stood up in Hong Kong! And throughout Africa!

THIS IS IT!

This is the GREAT AWAKENING!

Because this is not merely a human movement. This is a movement of the Spirit of God!

"the spirit of life from God entered into them, and they stood upon their feet!

This is a miracle!

This is the Great Awakening Ezekiel prophesied 2,500 years ago!

The end of the Beast system!

The Beginning of the Millennial Reign of Christ on earth!

God is pouring out His Spirit on all flesh! Just like Aquarius!

We didn't just stand up...

We stood up as a Mighty Army as Ezekiel 37 prophesied!

Joel prophesied about this amazing day too...

"I will pour out my Spirit on all people. Your sons and daughters will prophesy **(speak wisdom)**, *your old men will dream dreams* **(of a restored earth)**, *your young men will see visions* **(of a bright future)**. *Even on my servants, both men and women,* **I will pour out my Spirit in those days**. *And I will* **show wonders in the heavens and in the earth, blood, and fire, and pillars of smoke. The sun shall be turned into darkness, and the moon into blood,**

before the great and terrible day of the Lord come." (Joel 2:28-31)

This is WHY we are standing up... because so much is being revealed! To young, and old, and in-between! We are gaining so much knowledge and understanding, worldwide! We have seen blood moons, and catastrophes, and the sun turned into darkness. And we STOOD UP AGAINST THE NEW WORLD

ORDER!

With this knowledge, we are fighting for truth and justice! We are starting to rule in every place as if it is Christ Himself running the company, or the school, or the government office, or the court, or the religious group, or the entertainment production. Just as He said,

> "You have made them into a kingdom, priests to serve our God, and they will reign on the earth." (Revelation 5:10)

WE ARE STANDING UP! Ruling with Him on earth!

This is just the beginning! Every day will get brighter and brighter and better and better! Like the song, "... then peace will guide the planets and love will steer the stars. This is the Dawning of the Age Aquarius."

Isn't this AMAZING?! And did you catch the last part of verse 11? After we stood up...

> "great fear fell upon them who saw them."

The New World Order and their minions are in terror! This is **their** Armageddon! They can't stop us. And they know they are going to get the punishment they deserve. They are fighting to keep from losing power and going to prison! And worse. The Beast is desperate and trying desperate measures, but they won't be able to lull the masses back to sleep.

This is the end for the Beast and False Prophet.

> 12 "And they heard a great voice from heaven saying unto them, Come up hither. And they **ascended up to heaven in a cloud**; and their enemies beheld them."

So what does their rising mean? Many interpret this to be about Rapture/leaving earth. Nope.

Sorry to be so blunt.

But that's not it.

This is our LORD, raising His people into positions of authority all over the earth! He is raising our thoughts and our abilities and our courage. He is raising our awareness of Him and who we are, as His rulers of the earth. We're getting a RAISE!

The Deep State is out.

God's people are in.

And all the enemies can do is watch.

Haahahahahahahaha!

Clouds symbolize power and authority. Just like when Jesus returns "in the clouds," it means He will have GREAT power and authority, not puffy white evaporated water! Clouds are above humanity. Out of the reach of harm. In that way, God's people are being raised above humanity, out of the New World Order's reach, to rule the earth with justice!

> 13 *"And the same hour was there a great earthquake, and the tenth part of the city fell, and in the earthquake were slain of men seven thousand: and the remnant were frightened, and gave glory to the God of heaven."*

The earth quaking is Booms! The earth is shaking beneath them as judgment falls, and piece by piece their control structure is blowing apart! What if the first major boom brings down 10% of the New World Order? The number given here is 7,000. At that point many "gave glory to God in heaven." We know thousands of CEOs have been removed, and many turned evidence over to the DOJ. Any idea when the first earthquake took out a "tenth" of their evil swamp city DC? That boom was likely about a year after President Trump was elected, and almost half of Congress "resigned," and gave evidence to the DOJ in exchange for pardon. See #659, which said was the shot heard round the world. He called it Freedom Day. Not just for America. For the entire world.

You can see that pardon for yourself, because it was televised at the President's State of the Union speech in January 2018. Those who stood and clapped, and cheered USA! USA! USA! received a pardon. The rest sat and glared like spoiled children. They had their opportunity for pardon. They chose badly.

Day after day, piece by piece, their Evil Empire is being

dismantled and drained. Resignations of Congress and CEOs. Firings of top CIA, DOJ, and FBI Officials. Arrests of formerly untouchables power-players in Hollywood and the like. Seizures of Assets worldwide. By the end, it will be a total destruction of their Evil Empire!

FOUND THE 7th ANGEL TRUMPET!

Were you wondering where the seventh angel trumpet was? Remember in Revelation Chapter 9 we heard six of the seven angels blow their trumpets? But where is the seventh angel trumpet? Found it! Right here in Revelation Chapter 11! Since this trumpet blast is not with the others, it might chronologically come a while after the first six trumpets.

And do you remember how the final three trumpets were called TERRORS or WOES? I think of them more as SHOCKS or SURPRISES! Because the TERROR that comes on the Beast, is actually a WONDERFUL JOYFUL SURPRISE for us! So this seventh angel trumpet is also the third WOE/SHOCK/SURPRISE!!

We were told that this will shock the world! And the last Boom will be Magical! I think he is talking about this.

WE HAVE MORE THAN WE KNOW.

I think even we will be SHOCKED... in a VERY, VERY GOOD WAY! We keep being told to "Be Ready." That's why I'm so glad we are together on our Freedom Force Battalion. Even though there are some things I am not free to say, I think we are more ready than most.

THIS IS THE BEGINNING OF THE MILLENNIAL REIGN OF CHRIST ON EARTH!

> 15 *"And the seventh angel sounded; and there were great voices in heaven, saying, The kingdoms of this world are become the kingdoms of our Lord, and of his Christ; and he shall reign for ever and ever."*

Does verse 15 sound like a TERROR to you? It doesn't to me! The angels break into the Hallelujah Chorus! Praising the LORD that He has finally come to assume His role and begun to reign on earth!

But to the Deep State Beast Worldwide Criminal Mafia cabal, this is TERROR-ABLE! They are terrified of our LORD! And well they should be! He will destroy the destroyers with the blast of His Holy Nostrils!

> 15 "And the seventh angel sounded; and there were great voices in heaven, saying, **The kingdoms of this world are become the kingdoms of our Lord, and of his Christ; and he shall reign for ever and ever.**
>
> 16 And the four and twenty elders, which sat before God on their seats, fell upon their faces, and worshiped God,
>
> 17 Saying, We give thee thanks, O Lord God Almighty, which are, and was, and are to come; because **you have taken to yourself your great power, and have begun to reign."**
>
> 18 And the nations were angry, and your wrath is come, and the time of the dead, that they should be judged, and that you should give reward unto your servants the prophets, and to the saints, and them that fear your name, small and great; and should **destroy them which destroy the earth**.
>
> 19 And the temple of God was opened in heaven, and there was seen in his temple the **ark of his testament**: and there were lightnings, and voices, and thunderings, and an earthquake, and great hail."

And last but certainly not least, check out verse 19. Did you catch that? After the evildoers are destroyed and cast out, did you notice what happens? Everyone sees **THE ARK OF THE TESTAMENT** - or **THE ARK OF THE COVENANT**. The significance of that cannot be overstated. "Raiders of the Lost Ark" told us the Ark of the Covenant would be the most important archaeological discovery in the world. Well, the Ark of the Covenant has been found. And very few even know.

So where is it? I cannot go into detail here, but I encourage you to check the "Cataclysmic Find in Underground Vault" on the FreedomForce.LIVE social media link. Briefly though, on January 6, 1982, archaeologist Ron Wyatt discovered the Ark in the most amazing location. Twenty. Feet. Below. Where. Christ. Was. Crucified. Of course. Why didn't we expect that? And even more amazing, the Ark has blood on the mercy seat.

Again, the significance cannot be overstated. This fulfilled the prophecy, "He will anoint the Most Holy." And when Ron Wyatt had the blood tested, it was found to be alive! And beyond that, it had 23 female chromosomes, but only 1 male chromosome. This is the blood of our LORD Jesus Christ... fully man and fully God. The enormity of this is beyond words I can muster. What if that blood is used to verify the identity of our Savior?

Full. Stop.

Now do you see why I love Revelation 11?

Feel Free to Break into Song!

Hallelujah! Hallelujah! Hallelujah! Hallelujah!
For the LORD God Omnipotent reigneth.
Hallelujah! Hallelujah! Hallelujah! Hallelujah!
The kingdom of this world
Is become the kingdom of our Lord,
And of His Christ, and of His Christ;
And He shall reign for ever and ever,
For ever and ever, forever and ever,

King of kings, and LORD of lords,
King of kings, and LORD of lords,
And Lord of lords,
And He shall reign,
And He shall reign forever and ever,
King of kings, forever and ever,
And Lord of lords, Hallelujah! Hallelujah!

CHAPTER 13
HEAVENLY SIGN OF
THE SON OF MAN

This chapter has the most amazing heavenly star sign... the Sign of the Son of Man. I can't wait to show it to you!

But before I do, I think it will be helpful if I give you a summary of this chapter, because John shows us several visions and it can get confusing. Lots of movies do that. They show you scenes that are happening at different times, and you are meant to sort it all out in your mind. Revelation 12 does that.

I'll give a brief summary here:

The Sign of the Son of Man was the kickoff to the Great Awakening and the Battle of Armageddon. When the trumpets sounded in October 2016 and unleashed the winds of truth to humanity, there was nothing that would stop it! Though we don't see them, angels are fighting alongside us, as we battle these demonic forces. Holy angels help reveal truth. Demons are lying, trying to hold back the truth, and to keep the masses asleep. They are throwing everything they've got at us, with their 1/3 starry 33° minions, because they realize they can't stop the Kingdom of Christ from coming, and they are headed for the abyss. It says there was war in heaven, and satan was cast out of heaven and thrown down to earth. It's not saying satan was in heaven with grandma. This is symbolic language that satan was worshiped as the prince of the world, but the rituals and sacrifices have been stopped, and his powerful stronghold over earth has finally broken! He no longer holds that power over earth. That's why he's so angry, and pulling out all the stops! How many times have we been reminded that our battle is against SPIRITUAL FORCES? He's serious.

No doubt, our LORD is leading the Battle. He will defeat His enemies with an iron rod, and He will rule every nation. His Kingdom WILL be born on earth. And His precious bride, whether awake or asleep, will be protected for the period of the struggle, represented by 1,260 days. That is the angelic battle described in Revelation 12.

Finally, I get to show you the Sign of the Son of Man!

I've written about a lot of Bible prophecy. And about a lot of current events in the light of God's Word. But one question likely sticks in your mind.

HOW DO WE KNOW THE MILLENNIAL REIGN IS BEGINNING ("BEING BIRTHED") NOW?

Good question.

These worldwide events are wonderful and amazing, but,

REVELATION CHAPTER 12 CONVINCES ME THAT THIS IS THE BIRTH OF THE MILLENNIAL KINGDOM OF CHRIST ON EARTH.

God gave us a sign like the wise men saw when they KNEW FOR SURE Christ was being born. So buckle up to see that sign in Revelation Chapter 12!

Let's just say it. The whole book of Revelation is weird. So much imagery. So little time. Chapter 12 gets even weirder... especially to twentieth century Bible students who are not familiar with the starry constellations, or have been told to stay away from them altogether. John tells the story using a scene of heavenly signs. What?!

Remember when I said the LORD put the sun, moon, and stars in the heavens as **signs for us**? Now don't get worried. This is

NOT astrology. This is just like when the wise men knew by the stars that King Jesus was going to be born. It's called Biblical Astronomy.

*'The Lord put the sun, moon, and stars in the heavens for **SIGNS**, seasons, days, and years."* (Genesis 1:14)

*"He tells the number of the stars; he calls them all by their **NAMES**."* (Psalm 147:4)

*"The heavens declare the glory of God; and the firmament shows his handiwork. Day unto day utters speech, and night unto night shows knowledge. There is no speech nor language, where their voice is not heard. Their **LINE** is gone out through all the earth, and their words to the end of the world."* (Psalm 19)

In Psalm 147:4 we read that the LORD named the stars. Every culture has recognized the **names of each of the stars** that make up the constellations. That is how every culture agrees on what each constellation symbolizes. The stars' names determine what each constellation represents: a bull, a lion, a scorpion, etc.

The "**line**" in Psalm 19 is called the ecliptic, and that line goes right through the major constellations. The "wandering stars" travel along that ecliptic line, most of the time. Periodically the stars send us a God-ordained message, by creating a loop or a sine wave through a constellation. Amazing to see. Silently, day after day, the heavens are a Giant Sparkling Storybook speaking to us, revealing knowledge. We just need to learn to read it. See the FreedomForce.LIVE social media link for videos on Biblical Astronomy.

This is the beginning of Revelation Chapter 12:

*"And there appeared a **great wonder** in heaven; a woman clothed with the **sun**, and the **moon** under her feet, and upon her head a crown of twelve stars; and she being with child cried travailing in birth and pained to be delivered."*

The wonder in heaven is actually a sign including the sun, moon, and stars, and this is the first phase of four different phases.

The sign begins with the woman, which is Virgo.

The sun is shining on her shoulders.

The moon is under her feet.

And the crown on her head is Leo, with 3 additional stars, Venus, Mercury, and Mars.

The constellation Virgo represents God's people. The virgin. The bride of Christ. Right next to her is the King constellation, Leo – the Lion of the Tribe of Judah. And, yes, there's a dragon/ snake near Virgo's feet like in verse 3. The Archangel Michael is wrestling the dragon/snake, keeping him from the crown (the Corona Borealis).

> **NOTE**: If you think I'm making this up and want to know more, just search YouTube for "Mazzaroth" or "Biblical Astronomy" (Robert Wadsworth) and "Gospel in the Stars" YouTube site, and look up in the night sky! The Stellarium online planetarium and the Skyview app are helpful too. Also, check the "Signs in the Sun, Moon, and Stars" playlist on the FreedomForce.LIVE social media link. Don't miss out on your inheritance like I did for years! Those stars are for us! Just like the Wise Men understood Biblical Astronomy! They're not for horoscopes!

So what does the Virgo constellation tell us? Virgo represents God's people - all who believe in the LORD Jesus Christ, whether they are of the physical lineage or have been adopted into the family. Virgo is holding seeds, which is the Gospel we spread. Through the years, Virgo represented Eve, attempting to give birth to the savior, which she thought would be Abel, (who was actually killed by his brother Cain). And then Sarah and Rebecca and Rachel and Hannah and Ruth hoping to bring in the savior... and of course, the Virgin Mary, who did give birth to the Savior of the world. Virgo is crowned with the LORD'S Presence, shining God's light in a dark world, ruling over the dark occult (moon) under their feet, and being persecuted by the dragon, satan.

But Jesus spoke about **a special sign that we were to watch for**. **The Sign of the Son of Man.** And that is described perfectly in this twelfth Chapter of Revelation.

This sign in Revelation 12 includes the sun, the moon, AND the stars. Plus something extraordinary... 12 stars on her head, instead of the usual nine (which is the Leo constellation). And something SUPER-extraordinary... **a star in her womb**... being delivered after 9 months! Now THAT sounds like a really amazing sign... sounds like the "Sign of the Son of Man" that Jesus told us to watch for.

Do you want to see it?

THIS IS THE REVELATION 12 SIGN THAT APPEARED <u>ON</u> <u>SEPTEMBER 23, 2017</u>.

THE SIGN OF THE SON OF MAN

Isn't this remarkable?! What an amazing sign!

Virgo is the constellation that represents God's people – His bride. In this sign, Virgo is clothed with the sun, symbolically meaning she is filled with light and goodness. And the moon is under her feet, as if to say God's people rule over the enemy and darkness. And there are 12 stars on her head. Nine of those stars are Leo, which represents the Lion of the Tribe of Judah, who is our crown. He crowns us with lovingkindness and beauty as in Psalm 103:4, *"He redeems our life from destruction, who crowns us with lovingkindness and tender mercies."* As if that were not enough stars in our crown, the LORD adds three more stars in Virgo's crown. We'll get to their purpose in Revelation 14.

I watched the night sky as Jupiter (Melchizedek: Melchi =My King; Zedek=righteousness) entered the womb of

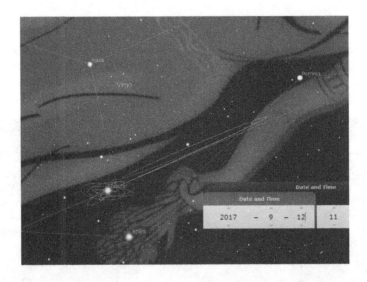

Virgo and saw it turn back around, and then make a giant loop! The loop took 42 weeks – the exact period of time for human gestation. What a sight! If you would like to see it, you can re-enact the sign on the free Stellarium.org online planetarium. I also have videos on my Freedom ForceBattalion. LIVE social media link on the Revelation playlist. Don't miss it!

Jupiter (Zedek in Hebrew) was "delivered" on September 9, 2017, and the exact Sign of the Son of Man appeared on September 23, 2017. This exact alignment of stars from Revelation 12 has **never** happened before, from 6,000 years in the past or 1,000 years into the future. How amazing is that?! The heavens are SHOUTING, "THIS IS IT!!"

September 23, 2017 was also a very special day on the Hebrew calendar. It was the first day of the Feast of Trumpets. The sound of shofars (Hebrew rams horn trumpets) was heard around the world, and signaled for all the people to gather together, connect with the LORD, resolve disputes, forgive and receive forgiveness. (For more on the Feast of Trumpets, check out the FreedomForce.LIVE social media link.)

Turns out, the New World Order knew all about the sign in the heavens. Make no mistake about it. They know the star signs very well. They just believe satan is in control and this signals the Beast's victory over humanity. They thought this sign would mark our defeat. They were wrong. Beyonce's Grammy Awards performance was part of their celebration, as she performed the star sign in Virgo, as the Queen of Heaven. They celebrated too soon. You lose, New World Order. God is in control!

I didn't know what it meant at the time, but now I am convinced the sign on September 23, 2017 was the Sign of the Son of Man in Revelation 12, and signals the Birth of the Millennial Kingdom Reign of Christ on earth! One evidence is that just after this Sign of the Son of Man, the people were gathered all over the world - the Patriot movement - Yellow Vests - Freedom Fighters! People rising up all over the world, fighting for righteousness and justice! And the great power and glory of Christ has been shown in how the enemy/New World Order is being defeated!

Our LORD Jesus told us to watch for the Sign of the Son of Man.

> "*Then the Sign of the Son of Man will appear in heaven, and then all the tribes of the earth will mourn, and they will see the Son of Man coming on the clouds of heaven with* **power and great glory**. *And He will send His angels with a great sound of a* **trumpet,** *and* **they will gather together His elect** *from the four winds, from one end of heaven to the other.*" (Matthew 24:30-31)

As if that is not spectacular enough, would you like to guess on what day Jupiter entered Virgo's womb to begin the sign of the Son of Man? November 9, 2016.

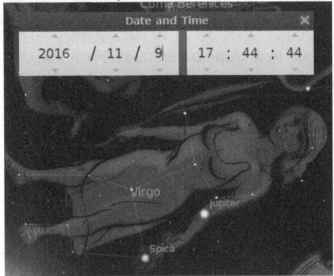

Does that date ring a bell?

That is the date the leader of the most powerful nation in the world was elected, President Donald J. Trump.

Full stop.

Take that in.

Really take that in.

Put the book down.

And take that in.

-

-

-

-

-

-

-

This is so huge that I feel that I should stop the book right here. But I'm not finished with Revelation, and there is so much more great news, so let's keep going. Just keep that nugget in your heart and mind as we go. Our President was elected on the very day this great wonder started in the heavens... the Sign of the Son of Man. The whole world has been shaking ever since.

After this sign was completed on September 23, 2017, the Beast/New World Order system began to crumble. It began with arrests of powerful players like Harvey Weinstein, and then a truckload of Sealed Federal Indictments (now 170,000+), CEO removals (now 12,275), and what is likely trillions of dollars of seized assets (now 1,390 pages). And of course, the Patriots! We began seeing coded intel in October 2017, giving us very important clues to break out of the matrix of disinfo propaganda. These clues help us see what has been going on behind the scenes of the criminal network throughout the world, and what patriots are doing to destroy it!

Now MILLIONS have joined the Patriot movement and we are spreading this information across every media platform, to overcome the propagated lies. Something very different - very earth-shattering and wonderful - is happening.

It is called **The Great Awakening.**

We are literally fighting the Great Battle of Armageddon against the New World Order Beast!

And President Donald J. Trump is leading the charge!

No doubt our President is anointed and appointed for such a time as this! If I get started on telling how wonderful President Trump is, I will never stop... so I'm going to focus back on the Revelation 12 star sign.

Another amazing factoid I discovered is that Virgo's crown is the exact shape of Queen Nefertiti's crown in Egypt. They depicted the lion's head as a snake on her crown. They knew about this star sign way back then. Wow.

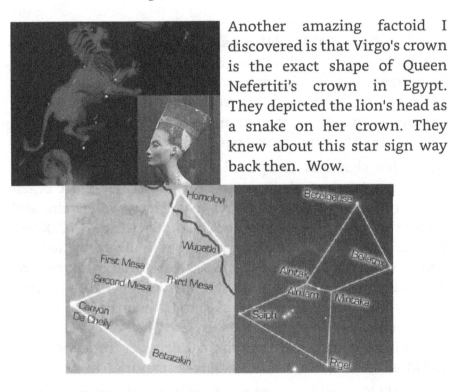

Another amazing find is this: Did you know that the pyramids are located throughout Egypt in the exact locations of the stars in the constellation Orion?

Wow!

And that the star shafts in the Great Pyramid of Giza aligned with Leo and Orion on September 23, 2017!

AMAZING!

There is a prophecy about Egypt in Isaiah 19:19 that I discuss on a video on the FreedomForce.LIVE social media link. I can't go into it here, but it is very interesting to learn how the LORD had the pyramids built as a sign for future generations... that's us! The Egyptians knew about this star sign way back then, and sent us messages that would not be lost! And the pyramids are still delivering the messages today, if we know how to read them. Wow!

Travailing in the Birth of the Kingdom of Christ

What does "travailing" look like? Shockingly, we don't hear many sermons on it (but we do hear messages on escaping in a rapture... but I digress.)

There is a beautiful passage in Isaiah 66 about travailing in the birth of this glorious kingdom. Marvelous! That, my friends, is what we are experiencing worldwide.

> 6 "A voice of noise from the city, a voice from the temple, a voice of the Lord that renders recompense to his enemies.
> 7 Before she **travailed**, she brought forth; before her pain came, she was delivered of a man child.
> 8 Who has heard such a thing? who has seen such things?   Shall the

earth be made to bring forth in one day?

*Or shall a nation be born at once? **For as soon as Zion travailed, she brought forth her children.**"* (Isaiah 66:6-8)

We believers are Zion - the City of God - and we are all travailing to bring forth this world of peace and justice we long for! Once you start looking for passages about the Kingdom of Christ on earth, you will find them EVERYWHERE! Definitely read Isaiah Chapters 58-66! Travailing (childbirth) verses are sprinkled throughout God's Word. Here are a few:

*"For when they shall say, Peace and safety; then sudden destruction comes upon them, as **travail** upon a woman with child; and they shall not escape."* (1st Thessalonians 5:3)

This is the destruction of the New World Order Beast!

*"For we know that the whole creation **groans and travails** in pain together until now."* (Romans 8:22)

*"And they shall be afraid: pangs and sorrows shall take hold of them; they shall be in pain as a woman that **travails**: they shall be amazed one at another; their faces shall be as flames."* (Isaiah 13:8)

This is the terror the New World Order is experiencing!

*"The king of Babylon has heard the report of them, and his hands grew feeble: anguish took hold of him, and pangs as of a woman in **travail**."* (Jeremiah 50:43)

The king of Babylon is the evil bloodlines, panicking!

*"My little children, of whom I **travail** in birth again until Christ be formed in you."* (Galatians 4:19)

We are travailing until Christ's Kingdom is formed in the earth!

Now that I have ranted about how amazing this heavenly wonder is, let's break down the rest of Revelation Chapter 12. What about this other sign in the heavens? A Great Red Dragon! We know one of the enemy's names is dragon. And in this passage, he's angry because we STOOD UP in Revelation Chapter 11, and he's on a rampage to destroy everyone in his sight! The stars (the rich and powerful) are already being exposed and cast down as casualties of this war. But the dragon is not finished trying to stop Christ's kingdom from being born!

> 3 "And there appeared another wonder in heaven; and behold a great red dragon, having seven heads and ten horns, and seven crowns upon his heads. 4 And his tail drew the third part of the stars of heaven, and did cast them to the earth: and the dragon stood before the woman which was ready to be delivered, for to devour her child as soon as it was born. 5 And she brought forth a man child, who was to rule all nations with a rod of iron: her child was caught up to God, and to his throne."

I haven't discovered a heavenly wonder regarding the dragon, but there are two constellations that certainly represent the enemy mentioned in this chapter.

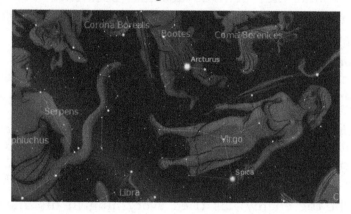

One constellation is Ophiuchus wrestling a huge serpent, to keep it from the corona (crown).
(see verse 14)

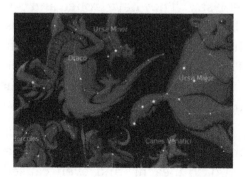

And one constellation is a dragon with a really long tail near the north pole. (see verse 3).

The "seven heads" of the serpent likely represent the seven world empires we discussed earlier in Chapter 2 of this book... each one using satanic power to try to destroy God's people. The "10 horns" likely represent the 10 divisions of oppressive authority that the Beast/NWO set up worldwide. This serpent matches the beast of Revelation 13 with seven heads and 10 horns. No doubt they derive their power from satan. The "seven crowns" symbolize that these empires consider themselves the ultimate authority, and they demand absolute obedience. The Beast directs their 33° minions to stop the Kingdom of Christ from coming to earth by any means necessary.

> 6 "And the woman fled into the wilderness, where she has a place prepared of God, that they should feed her there a thousand two hundred and threescore (1,260) days. 7 And there was war in heaven; Michael and his angels fought against the dragon; and the dragon fought and his angels; 8 And prevailed not; neither was their place found any more in heaven. 9 And the great dragon was cast out, that old serpent, called the devil, and satan, which deceives the whole world: he was cast out into the earth, and his angels were cast out with him."

No doubt the enemy has tried everything in his arsenal to prevent the truth from being exposed about the crimes that have been committed against humanity. They have shut down Twitter and Facebook and Reddit and YouTube accounts, shadow-banned posts, and given Patriots the dreaded name, "Conspiracy Theorists." They have trolled and cajoled and lambbasted truth-tellers. We are hardened veterans in this battle now. We laugh at trolls now. We love the smell of trolls in the morning. They have lied from every possible media outlet. It's actually funny now to watch them all spew the same talking points, like a band of robots.

They are trying to "devour" the Patriot movement with division and disinfo, and to silence us on social media. They've cried "Russia!" and "Impeach!" and even caused a worldwide "Plandemic". But we won't stop until we see them cast into the

Gitmo Abyss.

As verse five states, we have given birth to a man child. We elected President Donald John Trump, and he is leading us to victory as we are all raised up to rule and reign on this earth. There is no turning back. The enemy can not stop what is coming.

Judgment Day.

It is a hot war. Make no mistake about it. But we are protected for however long it takes. See verse six. Just as 1,260 symbolizes the great battle, we are protected during our time in this "wilderness" until He is revealed!

> 10 "And I heard a loud voice saying in heaven, Now is come salvation, and strength, and the kingdom of our God, and the power of his Christ: for the accuser of our brethren is cast down, which accused them before our God day and night. 11 And they overcame him by the blood of the Lamb, and by the word of their testimony; and they loved not their lives unto the death. 12 Therefore rejoice, you heavens, and you that dwell in them. Woe to the inhabitants of the earth and of the sea! For the devil is come down unto you, having great wrath, because he knows that he has but a short time. 13 And when the dragon saw that he was cast unto the earth, he persecuted the woman which brought forth the man child."

And there is no more place left on earth for the devil and his New World Order minions. We are casting them out, Out, OUT!

Yes, the battle is fierce. The enemy is throwing every evil trick at us, because he knows this is his last chance. He fights dirty with silent weapons like chemtrails (geoengineering) that cause many to have migraines, dizzy spells, seizures, depression, and other hormonal, breathing, mental and health problems. And the grey skies that go on day after day after day, like a grey-walled prison cell. (The plants hate it too.) The enemy fights with lies and lies and more lies.

But this is the Day of our Salvation! We have the strength of character, and the strength of numbers, and the strength of His Spirit. His Kingdom has come... and we are taking it by force.

We are overcoming by our very testimony, exposing every lie and every crime, demanding truth and justice on this earth!

We don't care what they say. We don't care what they call us. We don't care how they threaten. We are going to fight until they are defeated, no matter what it takes, and that is all there is to it.

14 "And to the woman were given two wings of a great eagle, that she might fly into the wilderness, into her place, where she is nourished for **a time, and times, and half a time,** *from the face of the serpent."*

What are these two wings of a great eagle?

I think that is America. Remember Daniel's vision of the eagle's wings that were plucked off the lion (England) and given the heart of a man to care for humanity? (Daniel 7)   God Bless America! Blessing and protecting people all over the whole world, now under the leadership of President Donald J. Trump, of course.

- Because of America, the North Koreans are being freed from the rogue Deep State government.

- Because of America, the Venezuelans are getting the support they need to throw off the tyrannical Maduro regime.

- Because of America, the Muslim Brotherhood has been defeated in the Middle East, and Syria is set free!

- Because of America, we are not going to war with Russia for another Deep State proxy war!

- Because of America, the Iron Eagle Nazi grip over the entire world is breaking!

- Because of America, all the captives- (political prisoners, slave labor, human trafficking victims, etc.) worldwide are being freed!

- Because of America, all the criminal Central Banks will be dismantled so the world will be set free from financial servitude!

And "Time, Times, and Half a Time"?

Time is 1 year. Times is 2 years. Half a Time is 1/2 year. So all together that equals 3 1/2 years. That equals 1,260 days = 42 months = which seems to symbolize the battle against the enemy, not a specific number of days on a calendar. Those are referenced throughout prophecy Scripture, and that interpretation fits every time!

What strange symbolism is next?!

> 15 "And the **serpent cast out of his mouth water as a flood after the woman, that he might cause her to be carried away of the flood.** 16 And the earth helped the woman, and the earth opened her mouth, and swallowed up the flood which the dragon cast out of his mouth. 17 And the dragon was angry with the woman, and went to make war with the remnant of her seed, which keep the commandments of God, and have the testimony of Jesus Christ."

Now THAT IS some strange symbolism!!

For those of us in the fight, what has the serpent spewed out of his mouth?

LIES! LIES! LIES! AND MORE LIES!!!

The enemy is continually trying to drown us and carry away our Freedom movement! But we are getting so much truth that their lies just get swallowed up and have no lasting effect!

HAHAHAHAHAHAHAHAHAHHAHAHAHAHAHHAHA!

The enemy is so mad because he's going down... and we are winning! Just like the LORD said in His Word! I don't care if he is mad. We are mad too, now that we have found out what the New World Order cabal has been doing to us! We win! You lose! Just like God's Word said would happen!

The Sign of the Son of Man did not end with the Jupiter loop in Virgo, and the angel messages of Mercury, Mars, and Venus. It actually has four phases. The four steps actually coincide with these four paths of Jupiter in the Sign of the Son of Man.

BIRTH PHASE
Trump Election & Qposts (Nov 10, '16 – Aug 31,'17)

JUDGMENT PHASE
Exposure & Indictments (Dec 25, '17 – Oct 15, '18)

WRESTLING PHASE
NWO Power Removed (Jan 10, 2019 – Oct 31, 2019)

DESTRUCTION PHASE
Prosecutions Begin (Feb 23, 2020 – Dec 25, 2020)

The first Jupiter (Melchizedek) path (loop like a slingshot) was in Virgo (Bride of Christ), representing the Birth Phase of the Battle of Armageddon. That was when President Trump was elected, the posts began, and the military operation began.

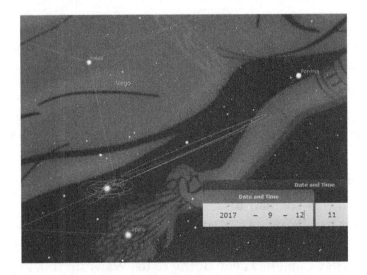

The second Jupiter (Melchizedek) path (loop) was in Libra (Justice), representing the Justice Phase of the Battle. That was when many indictments started to be filed, and the crimes of the

Deep State were exposed.

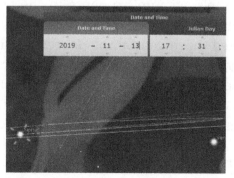

The third Jupiter (Melchizedek) path (zigzag lightning bolt) was in Ophiuchus (Serpent Wrestler), representing the Wrestling Phase of the Battle. That was when many powerful CEOs and DOJ, CIA, and FBI officials were removed, wrestling power out of their grasp.

The fourth Jupiter (Melchizedek) path (zigzag) which was in Sagittarius (the God/Man Destroyer), represents the Destruction Phase of the Battle. On December 21, Jupiter obliterates Saturn (satan), symbolically speaking.

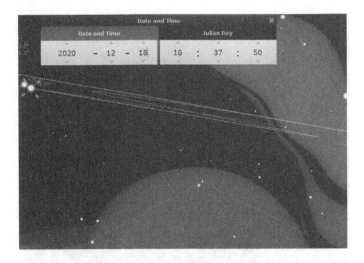

This amazing heavenly dance is powerful proof that the destruction of the New World Order we are seeing play out on earth, was written in the heavens for us by the LORD. And for us Patriots who are battle-weary, every beautiful heavenly sign encourages us to keep fighting, because our victory is sure!

PLUS...

Around the time of Passover 2020, President Trump mentioned his administration's accomplishments in the last 3 1/2 years. That prompted me to research the 1,260 days (3.5 years) prophecy. I looked specifically at the Hebrew Festivals and found something very, very interesting! It turns out that from the Feast of Trumpets on October 2, 2016 until the Feast of Purim, there are 1,260 days. The Feast of Purim celebrates when God's people were empowered to fight, and overcame Haman's evil execution edict. Sounds just like us, fighting the NWO's evil execution edict! WOW!

So I also looked at the prophecy Daniel was given, recorded in Daniel 12:11-12, to see if those dates possibly correlated. I had been trying to unravel that mystery for a long time! Here is that prophecy:

"There will be one thousand two hundred ninety days from the time the daily sacrifice is stopped to (for) the setting up of the desolating monstrosity." (Daniel 12:11)

In other words, it will take 1,290 days to stop the daily sacrifices that set up desolations on earth (think underground tunnels). These monstrous sacrifices caused the earth to be a desolate place, both spiritually and due to the devastating effects on children, their families, and world leaders. Precisely what the enemy wanted!

Check out what I discovered! From the Feast of Trumpets on October 2, 2016, to the Last Day of the Passover Week (Unleavened Bread) Festival on April 15, 2020, there were 1,290 days exactly! WOW! WOW!

We've been given hints that make us hope the monstrous sacrifices were stopped April 15, 2020! When I saw those days match, I almost fell out of my chair! I rushed to see where the 1,335 days prophecy would land! Here's Daniel 12:

"Happy is the one who waits and reaches one thousand three hundred thirty-five days." (Daniel 12:12)

Are you ready?

Make sure you're sitting down.

The 1,335th day is PENTECOST!!!

That is the Day of JUBILEE!

When God poured out His Spirit on the disciples!

When debts are paid and captives are freed!

That just CANNOT be a coincidence!

The Sign of the Son of Man started on the Feast of Trumpets, 2016, just before President Trump was elected, and coincides EXACTLY with Daniel 12.

Of course, this is confirmed by what we are seeing - the Deep State NWO being dismantled before our very eyes!

Our Day of Deliverance is closer than ever!

By faith, Let the Celebrations Begin!!

CHAPTER 14
HIDEOUS BEASTS

O f course, the Book of Revelation would not be complete if it didn't dedicate a chapter to the two most hideous beasts ever! That we are defeating, I might add! The Bible says satan is the prince of the power of the air, and he set up his kingdom on this earth. He is only able to do as he is allowed. The LORD is always in control - our wise and perfect Heavenly Father. The LORD allows the enemy to work through two main entities, through which they do satan's dirty work on this earth. This chapter calls them beasts because they are powerful and put people in great fear. So what/who are they?

Think LAWLESS. ANTI. OPPOSITE.

The OPPOSITE of the two witnesses in Revelation Chapter 11. Remember? The LORD has set up the Government and the Religious Institutions to be His witnesses of truth and peace on earth. So these beasts are the OPPOSITE of truth and peace on earth.

Revelation 13
1 "And I stood upon the sand of the sea, and saw a beast rise up out of the sea, having seven heads and ten horns, and upon his horns ten crowns, and upon his heads the name of blasphemy."

The Beast rising out of the sea reminds me of a science fiction movie! Like "The Creature from the Black Lagoon," or the sea monster in the "The Clash of the Titans!" So let's break this down into bite-sized portions.

When the Bible uses the word "sea," it is usually speaking of the sea of humanity. So that gives us a clue. This beast has seven heads because he considers himself to know everything, like God. But his knowledge only proves him to be a hideous monster with seven heads! And he wears 10 crowns on 10 horns, to rule over and enslave all of humanity. No doubt this Beast describes the tyrannical rulers of the New World Order. With their horns of power, they oppress physically, mentally, financially, politically, etc. They think they own humanity - that we are their "cattle" - their "food."

In order to enslave us "legally," they have utilized "the law of the **SEA**" or Maritime/Admiralty law, to remove sovereign rights of individuals and nations. The Law of the Sea is a body of international law governing the rights and duties of states in maritime environments. It concerns matters such as navigational rights, sea mineral claims, and coastal waters jurisdiction. The Beast of the Sea has used tricky Masonic legalese to create dry dock courts and corporations, to bankrupt nations, and rule the people as chattel via birth certificates. Search "War Castles Robert Leroy Horton," David Wynn Miller and Russell Jay Gould for more information on this. Even though these men helped to restore our rights legally, we still have to fight to enforce our rights. That requires prosecuting the Beast of the Sea, who refuses to operate under the rule of law. That requires Patriots.

The seven heads also remind us of other passages talking about seven hills, as in the seven hills of Rome. This Beast from the Sea stems from the brutal ancient genocidal Club of Rome, and continues to our day. The seven also reminds us of the seven kingdoms since Babylon (Revelation 17). The New World Order is a conglomeration of all those evil empires!

These seven heads attack the seven cultural influencers (gates) in order to infiltrate and destroy society: Government, Entertainment, Media, Business, Education, Religion, and Family.

The **10 horns with 10 crowns** call to mind the **10 toes** of Daniel's vision of Nebuchadnezzar's statue and the **10 horns** of the beast in Daniel 7, each 10 describing this tyrannical beast's power structure. These are 10 heads of power through which <u>they HAVE RULED</u> the entire world. On each head is a crown, because they demand absolute obedience to their sovereign rule. Notice I said <u>they HAVE ruled the world</u>. The whole world has been under their absolute authority, until now. The good news is that the 10 toes reminds us that their rule will soon end! There are no more body parts! In Daniel's vision, the stone cut without human hands smashed the evil empire statue to bits!

See the picture below. I believe it is a pretty accurate physical representation of the New World Order's 10 heads of power worldwide.

10 UN Worldwide Regions

The New World Order has operated through the United Nations... coming in peace, but using its power to kill, steal, and destroy. (UN is the Little Horn - See Chapter 2 of this book)

> 2 "*And the beast which I saw was like unto a leopard, and his feet were as the feet of a bear, and his mouth as the mouth of a lion: and the dragon gave him his power, and his seat, and great authority.*"

This beast reminds us of the four creatures – the lion, the bear, the leopard, and the monstrous beast - in Daniel's vision in Daniel Chapter 7.   These are the same beasts, all rolled into one! And to top it all off, they get their power from the dragon. In other words, they are satan-worshipers - Luciferians - Baal worshipers.

Horrifying.   Powerful.

    Ruthless.   Tyrannical.

3 "And I saw one of his heads as if it were wounded to death; and his deadly wound was healed: and all the world wondered after the beast."

We know that the New World Order has its origins in the Club of Rome, which morphed into Nazism/Globalism. A likely interpretation for this verse is that Nazis/Globalists caused the horrifying World Wars, and patriots fought to free themselves from their tyranny. The world **should** have defeated them at that time.   But, defying all reason, the real Nazis/Globalists came out of the World War mostly unscathed.   Only one of their heads was wounded.   This could mean their evils were exposed during WWII, but through fake news, others took the blame, and they skated! They   shockingly transferred their evil regime all throughout the world.   We have learned they infiltrated America through Operation Paperclip (scientists) and Operation Mockingbird (media). They infiltrated governments at every level and most had no idea! Truly amazing! They used their "defeat" as a springboard to launch worldwide domination. Their deadly wound WAS healed!

Sounds like a very logical and likely interpretation... and one they would prefer to hide through deception... which they have done by infiltrating seminaries.   And they would have gotten away with it, if it hadn't been for us meddling kids!!

4 "And they worshiped the dragon which gave power unto the beast: and they worshiped the beast, saying, Who is like unto the beast? who is able to make war with him?

5 And there was given unto him a mouth speaking great things and *blasphemies; and power was given unto him to continue **forty and two months**."*

As this passage says, they have spoken and done appalling blasphemies. Horrifying crimes against humanity. They have done this for "42 months"... (again, symbolically the period of struggle between good and evil), and we all know that their "power" is ultra-powerful! Controlling puppet government leaders worldwide, and every form of communication and food and all the central banks, etc. Total control worldwide.

6 "And he opened his mouth in blasphemy against God, to blaspheme his name, and his tabernacle, and them that dwell in heaven.

7 And it was given unto him to make war with the saints, and to overcome them: and power was given him over all kindred, and tongues, and nations."

No one could stop them. We have all come under their enslavement... and had to endure all of their mockery and blasphemy and tyranny... until now.

8 "And all that dwell upon the earth shall worship him, whose names are not written in the book of life of the Lamb slain from the foundation of the world."

Even though believers have had to live under the New World Order Beast's tyranny, we have not pledged our allegiance to its Anti-Christ culture. We made no secret oaths. We did not join with them for power and money.

9 "If any man have an ear, let him hear.

10 He that leads into captivity shall go into captivity: he that kills with the sword must be killed with the sword. Here is the patience and the faith of the saints."

John repeats how much patience and faith it will take, to suffer and wait until the right time to destroy the Beast. AGREED. Many have suffered and even died in this effort. Their reward is great.

While we are talking about the Beastly New World Order, remember the horrible offer satan made to our Wonderful LORD

Jesus Christ? He said,

> *"All the kingdoms of this world I will give to you, if you will just bow down and worship me."* (Matthew 4:9)

Of course, satan does not have this to offer, not the true Kingdom. But, Jesus flatly refused, and chose to go to the cross to suffer, pay our sin debt, redeem us from the curse, and receive the true crown as King of kings. The enemy made the same offer to the bloodlines of the New World Order. He would give them all the kingdoms of the world, if they would obey him (and pay a heavy price for eternity, which he failed to mention).

They said yes... and have been his minions ever since.

Ok. We have identified the Beast of the Sea.

Now let's tackle the Beast of the Earth.

> 11 *"And I beheld another beast coming up out of the earth; and he had two horns like a lamb, and he spoke as a dragon."*

First clue... this Beast comes up out of the earth. Remember the first Beast came up out of the sea? And we discussed briefly how that beast enslaved humanity by using the Law of the Seas/Maritime/Admiralty Law? The **First Beast** uses these piracy means to "legally" enslave the people, and then uses the **Second Beast** - the government and religious institutions - to lead the people to obey the rules, no matter how tyrannical the rules are! The government and religious leaders lend credence and authority to these pirates, so they can enact their theft and abuse.

The Second Beast is represented with lambs' horns, wolves in sheeps' clothing, appearing gentle, and putting the sheep at ease, while sending them to slaughter! These wolves are leaders we have trusted in government and religious institutions. Sheep are trusting, and cannot imagine that someone would knowingly lie to them, steal from them, and even kill them. But unfortunately, we have put our trust in wolves who do the NWO's bidding. How were we to know? Let's read on.

12 "And he exercises all the power of the first beast before him, and causes the earth and them which dwell therein to worship the first beast, whose deadly wound was healed."

The Second Beast works with the First Beast to accomplish their goal of bringing the masses into compliance. When it says, they cause everyone to worship the beast, think Obey. Comply. Follow. Believe.

The Second Beast makes sure the people do NOT, under any circumstances, identify and point out the crimes of the NWO. These wolves keep the people busy with ANYTHING but that. If a sheep starts to point out the crimes of those in power, they are quickly ridiculed and silenced, and punished, if necessary.

(Reminder: the deadly wound that was healed means that this beast had supposedly been eradicated, but has resurged! This is surely a reference to the satanic Baal Luciferian Set Death cult, which are Nazis. Their deadly wound of losing World War II was healed, and then these Nazis infiltrated the entire world.)

13 "And he does great wonders, so that he makes fire come down from heaven on the earth in the sight of men,"

14 And deceived them that dwell on the earth by the means of those miracles which he had power to do in the sight of the beast; saying to them that dwell on the earth, that they should make an image to the beast, which had the wound by a sword, and did live."

The Second Beast band of Government Officials and False Prophets have worked great wonders of diversion, better than any magician's trick. Whenever humanity has started to wake up, they have always diverted the people's attention, and they go right back to sleep. They keep the masses busy with religious busyness, and sports busyness, and political busyness. They keep the masses working 24/7, and focused on a thousand trivialities. They make sure the sheep never, Never, NEVER identify the Beast New World Order and fight them!

They lull the people to sleep, urging them to accept the sinking of their culture into degradation, promoting tolerance and peace, rather than urging justice on the enemy who is destroying their society.

For those who do want to fight injustice and evil, the Second Beast has them spend time on busy work, but never getting to the root of the problem... destroying the New World Order!

Until now! Thanks President Trump!

> 15 "And he had power to give life unto the image of the beast, that the image of the beast should both speak, and cause that as many as would not worship the image of the beast should be killed."

What is this?! This beast had power to give life to the image of the beast??? And the image of the beast should speak? That sounds like Sci-Fi for sure! Actually it is pretty obvious, when you think about it. It's got to be technology. We have little boxes of images that talk to us, and tell us exactly what the cabal wants us to know and do. We call them televisions, and laptops, and cell phones! They want us to believe and obey (worship) them.

That's why he says... TURN THEM OFF!!!

Will they really KILL those who do not worship the beast (listen and obey)??

Well, here's how it works.

Throughout the world, traitorous government and religious and community leaders have kept their fingers on the pulse of the communities they manage. Most controlled organizations have Masonic symbolism, such as glass-paned windows on signage or websites. (Windows symbolize spying... looking into one's soul, reminiscent of the first freemason building in America in Ephrata, Pennsylvania.) The masons have held the people in check, following the rules established by their lodges, which ultimately are funded and controlled by the New World Order. These traitors know those in their communities who rise up and speak out. Through social media, and church, and school, and civics organizations, they keep tabs on the trouble-makers, and ostracize or excommunicate offenders, bring false charges, or do them worse harm, if necessary. Many of them suppose they are doing God service.

> *16 "And he caused all, both small and great, rich and poor, free and bond, to receive a mark in their right hand, or in their foreheads:*

> *17 And that no man might buy or sell, save he that had the mark, or the name of the beast, or the number of his name.*

> *18 Here is wisdom. Let him that hath understanding count the number of the beast: for it is the number of a man; and his number is Six hundred threescore and six."*

That's what we will tackle in the next chapter.

666.

CHAPTER 15
SATAN'S MARK

I 've said it 1,000 times...

The "Mark of the Beast" is NOT a physical mark or a tattoo or an RFID chip.   That is Mass Deception.

(Do I think RFID chips could be used for evil? Yes. But is it the "Mark of the Beast"? NO.)

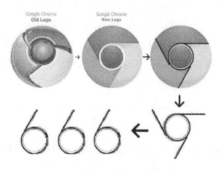

Let's focus on this passage about the Mark of the Beast.

15 "he had power to give life to the image of the beast, that the image of the beast should both speak, and cause that as many as would not worship the image of the beast should be killed."

At first glance, this sounds like we are all lined up, and if we will not bow to some strange image, we will be executed! Yikes!   (That's not it.) Remember, Revelation is chock-full of symbolism.

The image appears to be alive. And even speaks! So strange! Remember the Beast works under satanic power. And we have learned that the New World Order is the Beast, and that they get their power by allowing demons to live and operate through them. (Sorry if this sounds weird, but this is the spiritual battle that He keeps reminding us of from Ephesians 6 about putting on the full armor of God so we can war against spiritual forces.) This is a spiritual war, and we are dealing with demons who are operating through the New World Order minions.

What image "SPEAKS?"

Think.

We look at images all the time. Magazines. Movies. Internet. TV. MSM. I wonder if the LORD showed John a video. Imagine that! Someone 2,000 years ago seeing TV! And the description John came up with was "an image that speaks!" Sounds like what I would call it!

So, we all watch these images speaking every day. For hours a day. Those images speak and tell us what to think. They speak on behalf of the Beast. In that way, they "give life" to the Beast NWO. From MSM to politicians to Hollywood, to TV preachers. We have to believe what they say, or we are called "conspiracy theorists." They "kill" our reputation and our mental capacity if we question their narrative and authority. In that way, we have been "killed." We were neutralized from fighting against them. And some have been physically killed when they stood up against the "authorities." Either way, the New World Order has largely silenced their opposition. Until now.

> 16 "And he causes all, both small and great, rich and poor, free and bond, to receive a mark in their right hand, or in their foreheads."

So now to the MARK. We know from other passages that the mark is so evil that the LORD **MUST** punish it severely. That lets us know that the mark is NOT a mark that someone would take to simply save their families. God would not punish for that!

And the 144,000 in Revelation 14 have a mark, but no one expects that mark to be a tattoo or a chip!

Get it?! They are trying to throw us off the track! Those who fund and control seminaries, made sure the truth was not taught to the students. They have graduated and promoted those who agreed to their narrative. Especially about the mark. Because they don't want us to know what it is!

So what is it?

Ready?

It's really, really, really, really AWFUL.

It is the horrifying rituals to satan.

Terrifying. Demonic. Nightmarish.

From the Pits of Hell.

THAT is the MARK.

Those who do this evil have a MARK.

And THAT is why they will be horribly punished. Because once someone takes in the demons and does those demonic evils, they are too far gone. They have "blasphemed the Holy Spirit." They have sinned "the sin unto death." They must be eradicated.

And only those who have joined with the New World Order... and were willing to do these horrifying rituals to satan, have had the right to "buy or sell." Only "they" could become rich and gain true wealth. Only "they" could be in positions of authority and power. Only "they" could run corporations and become famous in their field.

Those who have joined the New World Order are from every social strata - rich, poor, small, great, every ethnicity, every nation, etc. Because the NWO needed minions they could control, who would do their bidding, all over the world.

Get the idea? This is NOT about needing a chip in order to buy groceries. This is about the world being controlled by evil minions of satan, while the rest of humanity are slaves. Of course, they would never teach that in seminaries, which are funded by the New World Order.

Getting the picture now?

The whole thing is One Big CON as in CON-TROL!

> *17 "And that no man might buy or sell, unless he that had the mark, or the name of the beast, or the number of his name."*

Whoever they were, they have shown by their hands (their actions), and their foreheads (their words), that they have given allegiance to the enemy. Because of their obedience to the dark side and its agenda, by committing unspeakable rituals, and harming innocents, they have received massive earthly rewards and power.

> *18 "Here is wisdom. Let him that has understanding count the number of the beast: for it is the number of a man; and his number is Six hundred threescore and six."*

Here is the verse about 666. John even told us that it would require <u>great understanding</u> to determine the number of the beast. It is the number of a man. We know that the number for God and perfection is seven.

777 is Perfect Completion. Perfect times three.

But the number of man is six.

Remember 1/3 (33%) of the angels rebelled against God and were cast out of heaven. And they fight every day against the non-rebellious 2/3 (66%) of angels and man. When the 33% (33°) pop up the 666 sign, they mean "We are here to destroy the obedient ones." 666 is their Battle Cry to Destroy Humanity!

THE MEANING OF 666

The New World Order has taken God's **sacred** institutions which were intended to benefit humanity, and perverted them for evil. Controlling Government and Religious Institutions by means of horrifying satanic rituals against the defenseless. That is Complete Evil.

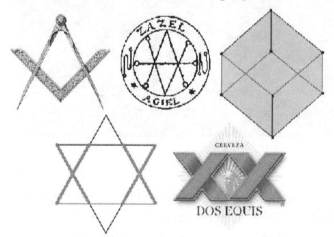

We've learned of their 666 symbolism, which they have displayed in many different forms. Do you see the 666 on the "W," the dot on the "i," and the "y?" They even hijacked the Star of David and the name Jew. (Soon the truth will be known. "Saving Israel for last." Israel is God's people scattered all over the world, all waiting for the Messiah, the Mashiach, the Mahdi, the Krishna, the Maitreya, following the LORD the best they can, despite their religious institutions being hijacked.)

The NWO's foolish pride in using this symbolism will be their downfall. It is their own admission of guilt!

To sum up this chapter, these two beasts were given authority to rule the earth. They are the complete opposite of the Religious Institutions and the Government which were intended to rule the earth for good.

These two beastly powers along with their minions make up the New World Order. Anyone who has stood up against them to get justice, has made very little ground. Through the NWO's secret societies, patriots have lost friends, family, power, health, jobs, money... even their lives. But the evil rule of the New World Order is coming to an end.

How on earth could these powerful, ruthless, crushing beasts EVER be defeated??

CHAPTER 16
144,000 AND TWO GREAT HARVESTS

For Patriots, get your popcorn! Chapter 14 is where we ride onto the scene along with our Great Commander! We will see more heavenly signs that match up in the battle against the New World Order Beast! And we will see the Judgment we have all been longing for!

Revelation 14
> 1 "And I looked, and, behold, a Lamb stood on the mount Zion, and with him **a hundred forty and four thousand**, having his Father's name written in their foreheads."

Remember the 144,000 from Revelation 7? Yep, these are the same ones! And look where they are! They are standing on the mountain of God's City, right alongside our LORD and Commander! They are the mighty warriors in the Great Battle of Armageddon! They are prepared to fight wherever our Commander directs!

> 2 "And I heard a voice from heaven, as the voice of many waters, and as the voice of a great thunder: and I heard the voice of harpers harping with their harps."

> 3 And they sang as it were a new song before the throne, and before the four beasts, and the elders: and no man could learn that song but **the hundred and forty and four thousand**, which were redeemed from the earth."

Patriots have a camaraderie that is so special, so unique, so powerful. It is difficult to find the words. We will always know, throughout all of eternity, that we stood shoulder to shoulder and fought valiantly in this battle. That we withstood the shills and the trolls... the attacks from family members and the fake patriots and antifa and all the brainwashed masses. We will remember the thundering rallies and the posts in the dead of night that kept us going. We will remember the fog of war when he didn't post for weeks. We will remember all the crazy memes that made us laugh, and all the beautiful videos that made us cry. We will know that no matter what, we rode right beside our LORD, and refused to quit the fight. No one will know the song of the 144,000 except true warriors in the Battle of Armageddon... like us, the battle-hardened Patriots.

> 4 *"These are they which were not defiled with women; for they are virgins. These are they which follow the Lamb where ever he goes. These were redeemed from among men, being the firstfruits unto God and to the Lamb."*

I doubt there any many virgins in the Army. This is not about physical virginity. This is about those who are pure in heart. Jesus said the pure in heart will see God. We see God. We see His Kingdom coming, and we are riding with Him straight into the hell of battle.

> 5 *"And in their mouth was found no guile: for they are without fault before the throne of God."*

"No guile" means that we are not deceivers. We are truth-tellers. Even if it makes people mad. Even if it gets us into trouble. We stay up nights and get up early just to get more truth out! And because of our relationship with Christ, we stand blameless before God. Now that's a miracle if I ever heard of one.

NOW.

GET READY.

THIS IS SO COOL.

THIS NEXT PASSAGE TALKS ABOUT ANGEL MESSENGERS.

THE BIBLE CALLS THESE SIGNS "GREAT WONDERS."

AND THEY ARE WONDERS.

A BUNCH OF 'EM!

SO GET READY.

FIRST READ THESE VERSES:

> 6 "And I saw another angel fly in the midst of heaven, having the everlasting gospel to preach unto them that dwell on the earth, and to every nation, and kindred, and tongue, and people,"

Everlasting GOOD NEWS for EVERYONE!

> 7 "Saying with a loud voice, Fear God, and give glory to him; for the hour of his judgment is come: and worship him that made heaven, and earth, and the sea, and the fountains of waters.
>
> 8 And there followed another angel, saying, Babylon is fallen, is fallen, that great city, because she made all nations drink of the wine of the wrath of her fornication."

The City of Babylon is not about a physical city. Babylon represents a city of evil, run by the devil himself.

> 9 "And the third angel followed them, saying with a loud voice, If any man worship the beast and his image, and receive his mark in his forehead, or in his hand,
>
> 10 The same shall drink of the wine of the wrath of God, which is poured out without mixture into the cup of his indignation; and he shall be tormented with fire and brimstone in the presence of the holy angels, and in the presence of the Lamb."

If you missed the section on the Mark of the Beast... check the last chapter. These people are in HUGE trouble. Nobody wants to drink the wine of God's wrath.

SO YOU'RE READY, RIGHT?

IF NOT, GET READY TO BE AMAZED!

Before the three Messenger Stars performed their messages, the LORD sent a huge warning to the NWO.

Remember the Solar Eclipse of August 21, 2017?

Guess where the sun was during the eclipse?

Right smack dab in the paw of Leo!

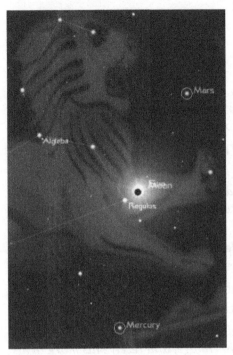

Wow!

That's so cool! The sun was shining in the King star - "Regulus," of the King Constellation - "Leo!"

All of these signs might be lost on the masses, but they are certainly not lost on the NWO Globalists. This was a warning that Christ, the Lion of the Tribe of Judah, the KING of kings is coming to tear the NWO satan worshipers apart! They know that solar eclipses are warnings of judgment!

EVERYBODY stopped to look at the solar eclipse, remember? Most likely didn't recognize what the sign meant though. Solar eclipses are signs for unbelievers. But this understanding has been mostly lost to our generation as a whole, and to the modern Church.

After the Revelation 12 Sign in the heavens appeared on September 23, 2017

three more heavenly signs of Revelation 14 appeared.

Remember the three stars - Mercury, Mars, and Venus - that completed the 12 stars in Virgo's crown? Well, now I'm going to tell you what they were for!

Messenger # 1

The First Messenger is Mercury and symbolizes speed, as in Speedy Judgment! After Mercury appeared in its precise placement for the Sign of the Son of Man, it continued its path, to fulfill its role of delivering the message of Revelation 14:7 – "Babylon is JUDGED."

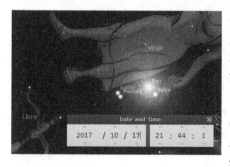

Mercury appeared next to Jupiter (Zedek), which represents King Jesus, received the message on October 17, 2017, and then...

on October 30, 2017, Mercury appeared in the center of Libra, the Scales of Justice constellation. There Mercury delivered the message, "Babylon is Judged."

6 *"I saw another angel fly in the midst of heaven, having the everlasting gospel to preach unto them that dwell on the earth, and to every nation, and kindred, and tongue, and people, Saying with a loud voice, **Fear God, and give glory to him; for the hour of his judgment is come:** worship him that made heaven, and earth, the*

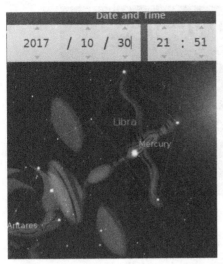

sea, and the fountains of water."

At first I thought that was cool, but maybe it was just a really cool "coincidence." Did anything "earth-shaking" happen around October 30, 2017?

SHOUT IT OUT LOUD!

That's when the Trump Team started posting, giving us the map about the treasonous and hideous crimes of the worldwide cabal!

That's what I call **JUDGMENT**! Because he has amassed a huge band of Justice Warriors who daily expose the crimes of the New World Order! The truth must come out first, for the criminals to be prosecuted and convicted. That is exactly what happened in October 2017!

AMAZING!

Messenger #2

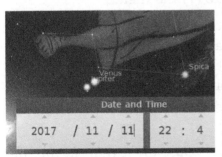

The Second Messenger is Venus and symbolizes God's love for humanity. After Venus appeared in its precise placement for the Sign of the Son of Man, it continued its path to fulfill the role of delivering the message of

Revelation 14:8 –

    *8 "And there followed another angel, saying, **Babylon is fallen, is fallen,** that great city, because she made all nations drink of the wine of the wrath of her fornication."*

Venus appeared right beside King Jupiter (Zedek), received the message on 11/11/2017, and then on

December 5, 2017, appeared right in the pincers of the Death and Destruction constellation Scorpio, to deliver the message, **"Babylon is Fallen!"** In other words, "We've got you in our grip New World Order!"

What happened on December 5, 2017? Remember this was the date the Keystone unlocked the door of all doors.

Q !ITPb.qbhqo ID: 7cfe10 No.38467☐ ▶   **269**
Dec 5 2017 16:01:30 (EST)

Key - unlocks the door of all doors (info)
Stone - the force / strength capable of yielding power to act on info
Key+Stone=
Q

ANSWERS

Q !ITPb.qbhqo ID: 7cfe10 No.38507☐ ▶   **270**
Dec 5 2017 16:06:17 (EST)

Adm R/ No Such Agency (W&W) + POTUS/USMIL =
Apply the Keystone.
Paint the picture.
Q

ANSWERS

In other words... We have it all. All the intel. And the ways to track in real time, all the Deep State Beast's treasonous crimes all around the world. The New World Order can no longer act covertly, under the cover of secrecy. Their Evil Empire is FALLEN!

WOW! (By the way, thank you Admiral Rogers!)

We are witnesses to the signs the LORD put in motion in the heavens thousands of years ago! AMAZING! This no doubt marks the end of the Beast!

Before we look at the third angel messenger from Revelation 14, there was yet ANOTHER sign! This was a warning to this worldwide network of criminals.

WARNING WARNING WARNING WARNING

TURN BACK NOW!

DANGER! DANGER!! DANGER!!!

"The LORD is, so gracious and patient, not willing that any should perish, but that all should come to repentance." (2nd Peter 3:9)

SUPER BLUE-BLOOD MOON on January 31, 2018

Three Signs in One!

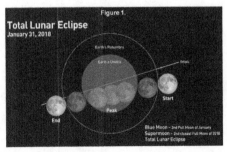

This sign was one of the last warnings to the Bluebloods.

"Turn State's evidence NOW!"

What are these signs?

BLUE MOON: two full moons in one calendar month, which usually happens only once every ~150 years.

SUPER MOON: the moon is closer to earth than at any other time of the year.

BLOOD MOON: the moon is eclipsed, giving it a reddish shade.

To have <u>one</u> of these signs appear is rare.

To have <u>two</u> signs appear at the same time is super-rare.

To have <u>three</u> signs appear at the very same time is

A SIGN FROM ALMIGHTY GOD!

Now for the Sign from Messenger #3

The Third Messenger is Mars, which symbolizes WAR.

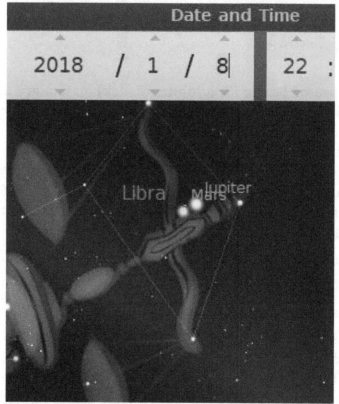

After Mars appeared in its precise placement for the Sign of the Son of Man, it continued its path to fulfill the role of delivering the message of Revelation 14:9 – "Come Out Now!"

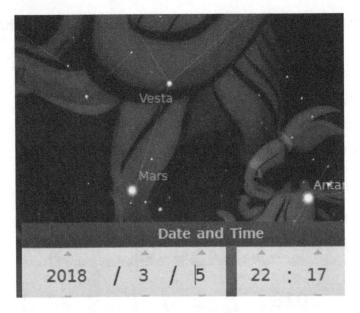

Mars appeared beside King Jupiter (Zedek) on January 8, 2018, received the message, and then on March 5,2018, appeared in the right thigh of Ophiuchus, to deliver the message, "Come Out from among them," which means, "If anyone is in league with the NWO, he will receive the wrath of God." What is the significance of Ophiuchus? Ophiuchus is the Great Serpent Wrestler who keeps the serpent from getting to the crown! Messages Received.

Messages Delivered!

Did anything remarkable occur on March 5, 2018? Boy did it!!!

This was the BIG news on March 5, 2018. What does this mean?

It means North Korea can no longer be used by the New World Order as a rogue CIA operation to hold the world hostage under nuclear threat.

Game Over for the Deep State. Come out of her. Turn State's evidence NOW.

Plus, this happened at the time of the Purim Festival... when we celebrate the thwarting of Haman's plot to annihilate God's

Anonymous 5 Mar 2018 - 10:53:58 PM

2b0ef287e47cb3064da23630eaee9a838861f0dc21a910d6
4f7e690c3c1c8c6bb.jpeg
>>562745

>>562749
Water.
Why is this event BIG?
What does it signify?
Why is NK out of the news?
As The World Turns.
Q

people!! (See Book of Esther.)

Let's read again that part of Revelation 14 with all the wonderful star signs we just witnessed, marveling that the LORD put these signs in the heavens, and worked these miracles before our very eyes. AMAZING!

6 *"And I saw another angel fly in the midst of heaven, having the everlasting gospel* (GOOD NEWS OF FREEDOM!!) *to preach unto them that dwell on the earth, and to every nation, and kindred, and tongue, and people,*

7 *Saying with a loud voice,* **Fear God, and give glory to him; for the hour of his judgment is come***: and worship him that made heaven, and earth, and the sea, and the fountains of waters.*

8 *And there followed another angel, saying,* **Babylon is fallen, is fallen, that great city,** (NO MORE COVERT ACTIONS – EVERY SECRET EXPOSED!) *because she made all nations drink of the wine of the wrath of her fornication.*

9 *And the third angel followed them, saying with a loud voice,* **If any man worship the beast and his image, and receive his mark in his forehead, or in his hand,**

10 **The same shall drink of the wine of the wrath of God,** (NO MORE HOPE OF HOLDING THE WORLD HOSTAGE TO NUCLEAR THREAT – SO COME OUT OF THE NEW WORLD ORDER NOW!) *which is poured out without mixture into the cup of his indignation; and he shall be tormented with fire and brimstone in the presence of the holy angels, and in the presence of the Lamb."*

AMAZING!   GLORIOUS!   VICTORIOUS!

11 *"And the smoke of their torment ascends up forever and ever: they have no rest day nor night, who worship the beast and his image, and*

whoever receives the mark of his name."

Please hear this:

The Mark of the Beast IS NOT A CHIP or TATTOO.

The Mark of the Beast is the horrifying blood rituals the satanists do. That is why they receive the wrath of God without mixture. (see Chapter 15 in this book for more on the Mark of the Beast.)

> 12 "Here is the patience of the saints: here are they that keep the commandments of God, and the faith of Jesus.
>
> 13 And I heard a voice from heaven saying unto me, Write, Blessed are the dead which die in the Lord from henceforth: Yes, says the Spirit, that they may rest from their labors; and their works do follow them."

Those who suffered in this battle, WILL BE REWARDED. FOREVER! Never doubt it!

These 3 Amazing Signs from Revelation 14 are:

Babylon is Judged

Babylon is Fallen

Final Warning to Repent

JUDGMENT DAY FOR THE BEAST

> 14 "And I looked, and behold a white cloud, and upon the cloud one sat like unto the Son of man, having on his head a golden crown, and in his hand a sharp sickle."

Of course, the one sitting on the white cloud is Christ – like unto the Son of man – like a human, but different. The God/Man. He alone has the power and the right to judge the earth. Because of His sacrificial death, He redeemed us from the enemy and He is crowned King of all kings! How wonderful is that! Our best Friend is the King of the world!

> 15 "And another angel came out of the temple, crying with a loud voice to him that sat on the cloud, Thrust in your sickle, and reap: for the time is come for you to reap; for the harvest of the earth is ripe."

Remember our LORD Jesus is the King of the World, but His attitude is always,

"I have come down from Heaven, not to do My own will, but the will of Him Who sent me." (John 6:47)

Our LORD waits to receive the message sent by His Father through the angel, before He begins to reap.

This reaping is the Great Harvest of believers.   The whole world will soon come awake from the spell we've been under, and everyone will know the LORD, as Jeremiah 31 says, from the least to the greatest!

"And they shall teach no more every man his neighbor, and every man his brother, saying, Know the LORD: for they shall all know me, from the least of them unto the greatest of them, saith the LORD: for I will forgive their iniquity, and I will remember their sin no more." (Jeremiah 31:34)

We are seeing it beginning even now!

16 "And he that sat on the cloud thrust in his sickle on the earth; and the earth was reaped.

17 And another angel came out of the temple which is in heaven, he also having a sharp sickle."

So, first God's people are awakened to hear the LORD... then we see clearly who our enemy is. And we crush the grapes of wrath together, as we pronounce judgment on them for their evil crimes against humanity.

*18 "And another angel came out from the altar, which had power over fire; and cried with a loud cry to him that had the sharp sickle, saying, Thrust in thy sharp sickle, and **gather the clusters of the vine of the earth; for her grapes are fully ripe.***

*19 And the angel thrust in his sickle into the earth, and gathered the vine of the earth, and cast it into the **great winepress of the wrath of God.***

20 And the winepress was trodden outside the city, and blood came out of the winepress, even unto the horse bridles, by the space of a thousand and six hundred furlongs."

This is quite picturesque language. What does it mean?

It is time.

These evil criminals are RIPE for judgment.

Imagine 170,000+ UNSEALED Federal Indictments.

Think of all the people who have been in these positions of authority over us, being brought to open shame before all the world for their treasonous, loathsome, hellish crimes against us. Imagine guilty verdicts being rendered for years to come, and punishment being meted out on those who were formerly the rich and powerful and famous.

Humiliated.

Stripped of every human comfort.

Scorned by all the world.

NOTE about the Hebrew Harvest Festivals: When Jesus came to earth the first time, He fulfilled the Spring Festivals of Passover, Unleavened Bread, and First Fruits. The Holy Spirit was poured out on Pentecost. Ever since, we have symbolically been in the summer planting. We've called it the Church Age. We've been going into all the world planting the Gospel seeds. At the end of summer, what do we have?

Harvest Time!

The Sign of the Son of Man, that appeared on September 23, 2017, actually began in motion at the Festival of Trumpets 2016, and awakened us!

This amazing four-phase heavenly sign is a Great Harvest Celebration! Just like the Feast of Trumpets, it is the signal for people to gather together like bundles of wheat, all over the world, and turn back to God!

Revelation Chapter 14 actually depicts two harvests. One harvest where the faithful receive rewards. One harvest where the evildoers are exposed and judged. That matches precisely with the harvest stories Jesus told. He said some of the harvest

END TIMES AND 1000 YEARS OF PEACE

produce was good. Some had to be thrown in the fire. At the grape harvest, grapes are gathered and crushed. No doubt the New World Order evil is fully ripe, and it is time for harvest!

Through all this upheaval, many are waking out of their slumber, and coming to know the LORD! That's the beginning of the Great Harvest! We are also seeing many in the New World Order who harden their hearts against the LORD, and will be harvested for judgment.

Remember, this is not the White Throne judgment. That occurs after the Gog and Magog battle, which is AFTER the Millennial Reign of Christ on earth. Right now we are setting up the Millennial Reign, setting things right, exposing those who have done evil, while removing them from authority, and revealing those who are Christ's true followers (Romans 8:18-21), and putting them in positions of authority all over the world.

CHAPTER 17
HEAVENLY SIGN OF
GOD'S WRATH

Friends, we who are awake have been shocked and horrified to learn of all the terrifying evil that has been done on the earth. Especially by the very ones we trusted the most! By the very leaders who promised they were looking out for us! We now know the truth, and we realize how dangerously, precariously close most of us were to complete and utter annihilation, and enslavement for the rest!

And we are seeing day after day, that the LORD is exposing the evil, and removing criminals from positions of authority, and installing His men and women into these positions! We are so very ready for the Day of Judgment to fall for all 170,000+ criminals of this New World Order worldwide network. This chapter is a powerful picture of our gratitude to the Lord for putting a stop to all the evil, and punishing the evildoers. Our PRAISE to Him will be Beyond Imagination!

Keep this chapter handy. We are going to need it soon!

Revelation 15

> 1 "And I saw another sign in heaven, great and marvelous, seven angels having the seven last plagues; for in them is filled up the wrath of God."

Here is yet ANOTHER heavenly star sign! From my research, I believe the seven angels are represented in the heavens by Pleiades, which is called the Seven Sisters, right in the heart of Taurus the Bull. Taurus represents our LORD Jesus coming to destroy the New World Order! Nobody can tame Him! He is

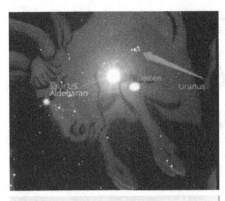

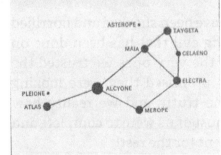

coming with Fire in His Eyes like the Red Bull!

Interesting that Pleiades is in the same shape as a map of the churches in Revelation 1. Pleiades is also mentioned in Job 38:31. It looks like a cluster of grapes, or a cup, representing God's wrath being poured out against this satanic evil.

You're going to LOVE this! A great wonder appeared right through the heart of Taurus during the week of December 12, 2018. I think it is the precursor to the sign mentioned in this verse.

Comet 46P Wirtanen went right by Pleiades ~December 12, 2018, as if our LORD Jesus was telling the whole world that He is filled with rage at what the New World Order has done, and that He is destroying them and their evil empire!

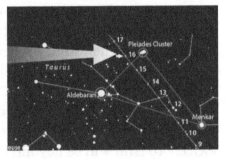

Next, I'm going to show you what might be the "Sign of the Wrath of God" from verse 1, *"I saw another sign in heaven, great and marvelous, seven angels having the seven last plagues; for in them is filled up the wrath of God."* On February 17, 2020, Venus left the ecliptic path, and in the Ides of March, entered Taurus on a rampage! Venus headed straight for Pleiades, and for four months is following its zigzag path through Taurus, the raging bull! History books will record better what we can only get clues on at this point. We believe that as Venus reached Pleiades, the abomination of desolation on earth was stopped. No more satanic rituals!

Praise the LORD!

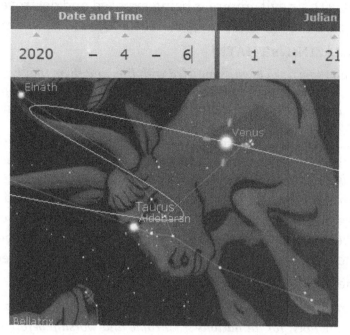

And the rampage continues as the NWO is being exposed before the entire world. The evil "Center for Disease Control," and the World Health Organization with their Pandemics and evil vaccines are being exposed! The United Nations that put a stranglehold on the earth is being destroyed! The NWO-controlled stock market and monopoly system is being turned over! The Masonically-controlled education system will never be the same! The President just broke the bloodlines' monopoly on the bulk power system, which is the beginning of free and safe energy worldwide! Soon the bankster-manipulated petrodollar and central banks throughout the world will be gone! And the wealth that the wicked hoarded will be restored to the righteous throughout every nation! Like a bull in a china shop, this heavenly sign is showing the cataclysmic changes on earth!

The "Sign of God's Wrath" in Taurus is coinciding with the Counting of the Omer for 50 days from The Feast of Firstfruits which is Easter (April 12, 2020) to Pentecost (May 30, 2020). Every day their evil empire is being exposed and destroyed. We just received a post and Trump tweet to "Drain The Swamp."

How AMAZING is THAT?!!

2 "And I saw a sea of glass mingled with fire: and them that had gotten the victory over the beast, and over his image, and over his mark, and over the number of his name, stand on the sea of glass, having the harps of God.

3 And they sing the song of Moses the servant of God, and the song of the Lamb, saying, Great and marvelous are thy works, Lord God Almighty; just and true are thy ways, thou King of saints."

After we see what great deliverance the LORD has worked for us, we are going to break into a Hallelujah chorus like you've never heard before! Just imagine hearing the effusive praise everyone will shout when we see our enemies judged, prosecuted, and punished!

4 "Who shall not revere You, O Lord, and glorify your name? for you only are holy: for all nations shall come and worship before you; for your judgments are made manifest to all.

5 And after that I looked, and, behold, the temple of the tabernacle of the testimony in heaven was opened:

6 And the seven angels came out of the temple, having the seven plagues, clothed in pure and white linen, and having their breasts girded with golden girdles.

*7 And one of the **four beasts** gave unto the seven angels seven golden vials full of the wrath of God, who lives for ever.*

8 And the temple was filled with smoke from the glory of God, and from his power; and no man was able to enter into the temple, til the seven plagues of the seven angels were fulfilled."

Don't be afraid.   Don't freak out.

These seven angels with the seven plagues are bringing utter destruction on the NWO, not on humanity! Did these four Beasts remind you of the four Beasts of Revelation 5?

*"The **four beasts** and four and twenty elders fell down before the Lamb,*

*having every one of them harps, and golden **vials** full of incense, which are the prayers of saints."* (Rev. 5:8)

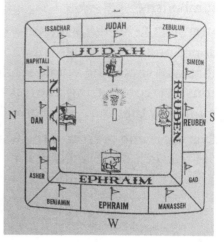

The four beasts represent the camp of the tribes of Israel in the wilderness. In other words, the four beasts represent God's people. In Revelation Chapter 5, they each have a vial, or a bottle, filled with prayers. But now in Chapter 15, we see those same vials filled with plagues of God's wrath! Wow! Our prayers, perfected by the Holy Spirit, are the basis of God's punishment for evildoers!

Every tear we have shed.

Every pain we have endured.

Every injustice they have committed.

The LORD remembers EVERYTHING we have suffered at their hands, and they will pay! The psalmist was telling the LORD all his troubles, and was comforted that the LORD remembers and even takes note of everything he had suffered. *"You number my wanderings; You put my tears into Your bottle; Are they not in Your book?"* (Psalm 56) Have you thought about that lately? The LORD has a bottle of the tears you have shed. He remembers what they have done to us, to our families, to our health, to our Countries, even when we have forgotten. He is NOT HAPPY that His children were treated this way.

An interesting side note is that during The Storm, we have seen a variety of vials. Expensive vials that the "elite" carry some strange potion in - likely "adreno-chrome." And celebrities wearing outfits with vials printed on them. Even a huge vial (vase) as a gift from the Chinese President Xi to President Trump. I bring that up just to point out the "vial" (vile) symbolism.

NUTSHELL: When everyone sees what these criminals have done, and the terrible shame and punishment they receive, that will shock the whole world. After this, no one will EVER consider committing the satanic rituals and crimes against humanity that the New World Order has committed.

Everyone who overcame the Beast will recognize that those who did this evil deserved God's most severe punishment. "Just and True are Your ways," they profess.

CHAPTER 18
THE STORM

F inally.

Finally.

FINALLY.

The Storm.

These past few years have been a really rough ride. Thank the LORD for this Day! At least we have known something of what has been going on behind the scenes, so we haven't been in the dark. Just imagine all those 1,387 pages of assets being seized! That's quite a vial! And imagine the CEOs and Congress and FBI, DOJ, and CIA and other authorities and leaders who have been removed worldwide! Now 12,000+!! That's quite a vial too! Months ago we were told about someone who constantly runs on their treadmill... but they can't run from justice! They are panicking because these vials are being poured out!

You and I hear the rumblings...

BUT THEY FEEL THE LIGHTNING BOLTS OF TRUTH!

THE STORM OF FEAR IS UPON THEM!

The angels who received those vials of plagues in Revelation Chapter 15, are finally given the command to pour those plagues out! (see verse 2) Don't focus on a chronological order, but on the continual barrage of destruction of the New

World Order from all sides. This chapter is meant to show us how these criminals keep getting exposed for their crimes, and are being incessantly pummeled with bad news day after day after day! The consequences are becoming progressively more intense. Some have repented. Many are still uselessly fighting back.

Remember, these plagues are for those who follow the beast – those who have taken the evil mark of demon possession and satanic rituals (hurting children in rituals beyond description). These plagues are not intended to harm those who follow Christ or for the brainwashed deceived masses. These plagues are specifically targeted at the New World Order!

These verses use strong symbolism, but each vial goes to the root of destroying their evil empire. Their health, their wealth, their sick pleasures, their prestige, their satanic worship, their kingdom ripped from them, and them ultimately being cast out to eternal punishment.

Revelation 16

> 1 "And I heard a great voice out of the temple saying to the seven angels, Go your ways, and pour out the vials of the wrath of God upon the earth.
>
> 2 And the first went, and poured out his vial upon the earth; and there fell a noisome and grievous sore **upon the men which had the mark of the beast**, and upon them which **worshiped his image**."

See it? Verse 2 clearly states that only those in league with the New World Order have the Mark of the Beast. The Mark of Pure Evil. We have been shocked to learn of their "chrome" drug of choice, which is harvested in the most demonic of means. And that the withdrawal from this "drug" has ghastly effects. This "grievous sore" is likely the just recompense in their flesh for the evil they have inflicted on others. They are living death; sleepless; constant fear; recognition of their impending eternal death; emptiness of soul; lifelessness.

> 3 "And the second angel poured out his vial upon the sea; and it became as the blood of a dead man: and every living soul died in the sea."

Many times the sea symbolizes humanity, but in this context it appears to symbolize commerce. They have lived extravagantly while the rest of humanity suffered. Now all their ill-gotten gains are being seized and their monopolies are being broken up, draining their finances. "Every living soul died" likely means every last business venture went bust. Business was dead.

> 4 "And the third angel poured out his vial upon the rivers and fountains of waters; and they became blood."

Rivers and fountains usually symbolize pleasure. The NWO's pleasures died too. These people are sick, and they have sick pleasures. In verse 4, the angel's vial prevents them from fulfilling those sick pleasures any more. Thank God!

Fountains also represent joy and satisfaction and refreshment, but there is none for them. Constant Thirst. No joy. No peace. Only the constant agonizing reminder of judgment. God's vengeance, and death - symbolized by blood.

> 5 "And I heard the angel of the waters say, You are righteous, O Lord, which are, and was, and shall be, because you have judged thus. 6 For they have shed the blood of saints and prophets, and you have given them blood to drink; for they are worthy. ("they deserve it!") 7 And I heard another out of the altar say, Even so, Lord God Almighty, true and righteous are thy judgments."

Just in case anyone feels sorry for these satanists, the angels remind us that they deserve every drop of the wrath of God they are getting. As more and more learn of their horrifying crimes, especially against children, "celebrities" will lose every last bit of prestige they had, and will be held in utter contempt forever. Therefore heaven and earth will stand in wholehearted agreement that the Beast New World Order is worthy of God's harshest judgment. Get ready for four more vials, which God is true and righteous to mete out!

> 8 "And the fourth angel poured out his vial upon the sun; and power was given unto him to scorch men with fire. 9 And men were scorched with great heat, and blasphemed the name of God, which hath power over these plagues: and they repented not to give him glory."

What could the sun represent? I have a few ideas. Scorching misery; Fear beating down on them like the summer sun; No relief from the terror. Most would rather be miserable than humble themselves, turn to God, and turn from evil. Of course, they would be risking their lives to give evidence to the authorities at this point. I think the New World Order minions are piping hot because of all their evil deeds being exposed, and their inability to stop Trump and us, and the criminal investigations, and the daily revelations on social media. And they are no doubt harassed by demonic tormentors who are also angry, as well as false friends, as they all blame each other for what is happening. Can you just imagine the outrage and the blasphemous arguments they are having with each other? That's where you'd see some fiery Armageddon fireworks! I do not feel sorry for them in the slightest. If I start to feel mercy toward them, I remember the children they have gleefully tortured. "LORD, pour out the vials!"

> 10 "And the fifth angel poured out his vial upon the seat of the beast; and his kingdom was full of darkness; and they gnawed their tongues for pain."

This vial is poured out on the SEAT of the BEAST. That has to be the SEAT of POWER. Finally, with the 5th vial, the Evil Empire's power structure is dismantled and destroyed. Each day the NWO power is being destroyed. Spiritually they are in the darkness of sin. Of course they have no comfort of God's presence or any true peace. The Deep State is operating in darkness, because their communication lines have been shut down. They have to resort to posting cryptic messages on social media! And now THEY are the ones constantly under surveillance! I'm sure they are so angry and frustrated!

> 11 "And blasphemed the God of heaven because of their pains and their sores, and repented not of their deeds."

On top of the loss of their wealth and their pleasures and their prestige, and any vestige of peace, they are aging rapidly with physical maladies brought on by their satanic rituals, e.g. their withdrawal symptoms from "chrome," and likely severe demonic oppression.

As the angels said, "THEY DESERVE IT!"

And we #EnjoyTheShow and Laugh and Laugh and Laugh! Bring on the next vial!

> 12 "And the sixth angel poured out his vial upon the great river Euphrates; and the water thereof was dried up, that the way of the kings of the east might be prepared."

At first, I thought this vial was the NWO-initiated immigrant invasion that caused displacement of homelands, and upheaval worldwide. But after closer examination, I realize that since the vials are answers to our prayers for justice and rescue, each vial is destroying the Beast's kingdom on earth.

So what clues do we find in this passage? Let's consider "the kings of the east." Who are they? We know the Wise Men at Jesus' birth were called "the kings of the east." And we know that they traveled westward to Bethlehem for Christ's first advent. So what could these "kings of the east" be preparing for? To have the great river Euphrates dried up so there is nothing in their way? Could it be Christ's SECOND ADVENT? I think we are onto something! We know we have seen the "Sign of the Son of Man" which says we will see the Son of Man coming in power and great glory. I think that's it! And just wait until we get to verse 15!

No doubt, it will be a very terrible vial for the NWO to see the kingdom ripped away from them, and given to those who will produce its fruits. When they see this happening, they pull out all the stops!

> 13 "And I saw three unclean spirits like frogs come out of the mouth of the dragon, and out of the mouth of the beast, and out of the mouth of the false prophet."

You know who the unclean spirits like frogs out of the mouths of the dragon, the beast, and the false prophet are. No need for me to even type it out. Shout it with me, Patriots! FAKE

185

NEWS! Unclean Spirits like Frogs. Yep, that's got to be all the lies we hear from every direction... all in lock step! Deception from the pits of hell, straight from the 2 a.m. talking points sent out to every media outlet and religious organization that works for the New World Order. There's something about frogs. One might be fine. For a few minutes. But when you have hundreds of them, all around, they are dirty and gross and disgusting. And all you want to do is get rid of them! That's the bulk of Mainstream Media, and Politcians, the Hollyweird Harlots, and Sports figures, and Fake Preachers that flap their froggy gums. Ew! Out! Out! OUT!

14 "For they are the spirits of devils, working miracles, which go forth unto the kings of the earth and of the whole world, to gather them to the battle of that great day of God Almighty."

What miracles have they worked? That the masses have listened to their drivel and lapped it up! We are literally at war against their lying Socialist Marxist Cabal propaganda army. We knock out each lie with a handy dandy meme, while they are left standing there with their mouths hanging open. He just posted that we are winning the information war! When this happens, when they have to pull out the froggy desperate deceptions, you know the war is almost over. Don't believe me. Just read the next verse!

15 "Behold, I come as a thief. Blessed is he that watches, and keeps his garments, lest he walk naked, and they see his shame."

Please read this verse carefully.

"I come as a thief."

"I come as a THIEF."

Thieves do not announce their arrival.

Real thieves don't come in the way you would expect with a bandana over their face and with guns blazing. Thieves are sneaky. They come where no one is watching.

So is our LORD.

That is what this verse is saying.

Our LORD Jesus is sneaky as a thief.

He will come in an unexpected way.

That's what this verse says.

And that we need to WATCH. Or we will be ashamed.

There are many Bible teachers who have no idea that this is the Great Day of the LORD.

They have no idea this is the Great Awakening.

They have no idea we are fighting Armageddon.

Explain that to me. I can't explain it. Except that they are not watching. And one day, everyone will see their shame... I didn't write that.

So... we know this is Armageddon and the Great Day of the LORD.

What else might we not be aware of?

Something that is right under our noses.

Like a thief picking our pockets and we don't even notice?

But I'm not going to tell you.

Except to say that <u>our LORD is sneaky as a thief.</u>

Watch.

And that's all I'm going to say about that.

> 16 "And he gathered them together into a place called in the Hebrew tongue Armageddon.
>
> 17 And the seventh angel poured out his vial into the air; and there came a great voice out of the temple of heaven, from the throne, saying, It is done.
>
> 18 And there were voices, and thunders, and lightnings; and there was a great earthquake, such as was not since men were upon the earth, so mighty an earthquake, and so great.
>
> 19 And the great city was divided into three parts, and the cities of the nations fell: and great Babylon came in remembrance before God, to

give unto her the cup of the wine of the fierceness of his wrath.
20 And every island fled away, and the mountains were not found."

WOW!

An earthquake - and the city divided into three parts, - and the islands and mountains disappearing - and the huge hailstones... What a show!

These are not physical, geological happenings.

Nope!

Nope!

Nope!

They represent the utter and complete devastation and destruction of the Beast, False Prophet, and the Harlot.

What do the *Voice, Thunders, Lightnings, and Earthquakes* represent?

God's judgment raining down on the NWO, shaking and utterly destroying them forever! Rumor has it, on March 30, 2020, Elizabeth II, the Queen of England, was proven in court to be illegitimate. Elizabeth moved out of Buckingham Palace and has lived in Windsor Palace ever since. Quite an earthquake!

What does the *City Divided in Three Parts* represent?

The NWO's three-sided pyramid of evil will collapse, never to rise again!

The Vatican, seat of spiritual control, gone.

The City of London, seat of financial control, gone.

Washington DC, seat of military control, gone.

What do the *Islands and Mountains* represent?

The smallest satanic minions all the way to the most powerful bloodline "godfathers" of the New World Order will be gone, never to harm humanity again!

What do the *Hailstones* represent?

That the NWO will be crushed like grapes of wrath under God's judgment.

What a powerful image these verses paint of what will happen to the Beast, the False Prophet, and the Harlot! Make no mistake about it. They will be destroyed completely. And we will have peace on earth. Feel free to break into the Hallelujah Chorus again!

By the way, we haven't gone into detail about who the "Harlot" is. I know you were too polite to ask. So, the LORD made an entire chapter on it. And that's next.

CHAPTER 19
HARLOTS DO ANYTHING FOR MONEY

R eady to hear about another player?! And this one really is a player! Sorry to be crass, but if you want to know who the Harlot of Revelation is, just realize what a harlot does - literally ANYTHING for money. These people are fully committed to doing whatever they are told to do, in order to get whatever they want. And... they give hearty approval to those who do the same. Rebellious. Lawless. Selfish. Proud. Greedy. Lustful. Willing to Lie, Deceive, Steal, Cheat, even Terrorize and Kill to get what they want.

The Harlot fully supports the Beast New World Order, but the Harlot does not have intrinsic financial or authoritative power like the Beast. So it is strange that verse 18 says she actually **rules** over the Beast. That is because the Harlot is powerful due to the great number in their ranks, and the deception and evil they carry out. The Beast *needs* the Harlot, to work their evil plan.

The Beast and the Harlot don't care about each other. They only use each other to get what they want. Those in power have no respect for the Harlot and will just toss her aside when they are finished with her. Hence the name. So who is this Harlot?

Just think of those who help the New World Order accomplish their evil agenda. I'm not creating this list below to freak you out. I'm just trying to help you realize WHO the Harlot is, and where you'll find them. They have predominantly been in leadership positions throughout the world. (Don't worry. THEY'RE BEING REMOVED, AND WILL BE PROSECUTED AND HELD TO PAY FOR THEIR CRIMES.)

MSM (Mainstream Media) - Think Producers of Radio, TV, Newspapers, Magazines, Social Media sites

Entertainment Industry - Think Producers of Hollywood, Music, Technology, Movies

Education Institutions - Think Directors of Masonic State Education Agencies, Professors, Administrators, School Boards, Masonic Textbook Producers

Medical Institutions - Think Drug Manufacturers, Organ Harvesting, Cancer Industry, Masonic Medical Professors, Criminal Coroners

Puppet Politicians - Politicians throughout every Branch of Federal, State, and Local Governments

Puppet Government Leaders - Think Judges, Police Chiefs, and District Attorneys

Puppet Government Justice Agencies - think CIA, DOJ, FBI, Intelligence Agencies Worldwide

Puppet Government Agencies - think FDA that is supposed to protect our food, water & drugs, CDC and WHO (Vaccines & Pharmaceuticals & Diseases), Departments of Defense, Energy etc.

Banks - Think Central and National Bank Directors, and the Stock Market to manipulate the money system and revolving credit debt enslavement

United Nations Puppets - Think of the Officials who drain each Country's natural resources, control their media and education and healthcare, enforce NWO propaganda, and foment wars

Tech Giants - Think Controllers of Facebook, Twitter, Google, YouTube, Amazon, and other CIA Spy Software and Voting machines

Corporations - Think of NWO minions who produce our foods, pesticides, home goods, building products, all filled with who knows what, plus global corporations that ship goods worldwide with little or no restrictions on their contents

Medical Associations - Think "experts" promoting Big Pharma, Big Cancer, Big Disease

Secret Societies - Think local leaders controlling local communities, filling every board.

So, with that in mind, it's time to dive into Revelation Chapter 17. Let's go!

Revelation 17

1 "And there came one of the seven angels which had the seven vials, and talked with me, saying unto me, Come here; I will show you the judgment of the great harlot that sits upon many waters."

What strange imagery... "the harlot sits upon many waters." You probably figured out the Harlot is people selected from all of humanity - every nation, every language, every ethnicity, every social strata, infiltrating every organization. (see Revelation 17:15)

2 "With whom the kings of the earth have committed fornication, and the inhabitants of the earth have been made drunk with the wine of her fornication."

And these people are willing to do literally ANYTHING for the New World Order. They are addicted to - drunk on - the power and money and prestige. Many do have literal orgies, but I think this verse is symbolizing their delight in stealing from and abusing the unsuspecting world. They have laughed and laughed and laughed at how we have believed whatever they said and trusted them... while they were sticking it to us! I also give room for useful idiots who are unwitting participants.

*3 "So he carried me away in the spirit into the wilderness: and I saw a **woman sit upon a scarlet colored beast**, full of names of blasphemy,* *having seven heads and ten horns.*

4 And the woman was arrayed in purple and scarlet color, and decked with gold and precious stones and pearls, having a golden cup in her hand full of abominations and filthiness of her fornication."

This Beast is the same Tyrannical Beast of the Sea described in Revelation Chapter 13. And the ones on the list you just read, ride in this evil system where they get their illicit power and riches... either from well-paid employment positions, or drug money, or Hollywood, or bribes, or political slush funds... or straight from the New World Order bloodline players. (See Fritz Springmeir's book.) And to prove their loyalty to each other, many at the top participate in filthy abominations that I would rather not write about. These people are sick.

5 "And upon her forehead was a name written, Mystery, Babylon The Great, The Mother Of Harlots And Abominations Of The Earth."

I've heard some identify certain nations, (i.e. America) as Mystery Babylon the Great.

Nope.

That's just way too simplistic.

"Mystery, Babylon the Great, The Mother Of All Harlots And Abominations Of The Earth" includes all these evildoers in this secret cabal, who have joined with the New World Order. Soon they will not be able to harm us, from where they are going.

6 "And I saw the woman drunken with the blood of the saints, and with the blood of the martyrs of Jesus: and when I saw her, I wondered greatly.

7 And the angel said unto me, Wherefore did you marvel? I will tell you the mystery of the woman, and of the beast that carried her, which has the seven heads and ten horns.

*8 **The beast that you saw was, and is not**; and shall ascend out of the bottomless pit, and go into perdition: and they that dwell on the earth shall wonder, whose names were not written in the book of life from the foundation of the world, when they behold the **beast that was, and is not, and yet is**."*

What an interesting statement from the angel! He said that

during the time when John was given this vision, the Beast did not exist. As evil as the societies were in John's day, they did not sink to the depths of evil that the New World Order has sunk to in our day! As this verse says, they are drunk on their power to do evil! The Beast had formerly been on earth, but had been eliminated. I believe the angel is talking about the evil Baal/Baphomet/Ra/Luciferian/Set Death Cult, with all its extreme rituals that turn the stomach, and are the thing of nightmares.

Remember when the Prophet Elijah went against Jezebel and Ahab? And the 450 prophets of Baal were killed? (1st Kings 18) That might be what John means when he says, "the beast **IS NOT**," because the Prophet Elijah eliminated the Baal Luciferian Death Cult from the earth. At least it was eliminated from Israel. The main point is, that this ancient satanic religion has come back with a vengeance in our day. And most of us didn't even know until recently, that the world powers operated under this evil satanic system. But now that we know, we are going to end it, once and for all!

9 "And here is the mind which has wisdom. The seven heads are seven mountains, on which the woman sits."

COMPLICATED RIDDLE DECODED!

Pretty much everyone agrees that the seven mountains symbolize Rome. I agree, and would add, that "Rome" is the evil Club of Rome that transformed into the New World Order which has ruled the entire world with an iron fist using central banks, and drug and human trafficking.

*10 "And there are **seven kings: five are fallen**, and **one is**, and the other is **not yet come**; and when he comes, he must continue a short space.*

*11 And **the beast that was**, and **is not**, even **he is the eighth**, and **is of the seven**, and goes into perdition."*

Verses 10 and 11 are a bit more complicated and will take a little time to "decode" this riddle. I will give you my thoughts, and you can research more on your own, as I always encourage you to do.

Always study and research and pray for revelation.

First, I believe kings actually symbolizes KINGDOMS or EMPIRES. What seven Kingdoms have ruled the known world throughout time?

1 - Egyptian Empire **FALLEN**

2 - Babylonian Empire **FALLEN**

3 - Median Empire **FALLEN**

4 - Persian Empire **FALLEN**

5 - Greek Empire **FALLEN**

6 - Roman Empire **NOW IS** (during John's time)

7 - "Holy" Roman Empire **NOT YET COME** (during John's time),

CONTINUE A SHORT SPACE

8 – New World Order **IS OF THE 7 –AND GOES TO PERDITION.**

That took some doing to figure out, so take some time to make sure you understand the eight empires.

So let's decode this Eighth Evil Empire.

This is what the angel told John:

> *"the beast that was, and is not,*
>
> (the Egyptian Luciferian Set Death Cult mentioned earlier, that had been eliminated)
>
> *"even he is the eighth, and is of the seven."*
>
> (the eighth empire (NWO) is a resurgence of the seven - likely the Egyptian/Babylonian/Roman Empires with their satanic Baal/Luciferian/Set/Death cult)
>
> *and goes into perdition."*
>
> (will be judged and cast into the abyss).

I believe that is a pretty likely decode of those verses. Especially as it fits with the following verses about their power structure.

> *12 "And the ten horns which you saw are ten kings* (kingdoms/

empires), *which have received no kingdom as yet; but receive power as kings one hour with the beast.*

13 These have one mind, and shall give their power and strength unto the beast."

These are the same **10 toes** – **10 horns** – **10 kings** (kingdoms) that the LORD keeps telling us about. I believe these are the 10 regions managed by the United Nations, under the authority of the New World Order. They work together in lock step for world domination/control for one hour - which means, for a short period of time. The United Nations originated 75 years ago, April 25, 1945. It appears their day is over. Thank God.

UNITED NATIONS 10 REGIONS WORLD DOMINATION

10 UN Worldwide Regions

All those Saturday morning cartoons that we thought were joking around about world domination... WERE SERIOUS!!

14 "These shall make war with the Lamb, and the Lamb shall overcome them: for he is Lord of lords, and King of kings: and they that are with him are called, and chosen, and faithful."

What an honor to fight in this epic battle!

We are Called. Chosen. And Faithful.

15 "And he says unto me, The waters which you saw, where the harlot sits, are peoples, and multitudes, and nations, and tongues.

16 And the ten horns which you saw upon the beast, these shall hate the harlot, and shall make her desolate and naked, and shall eat her flesh, and burn her with fire.

17 For God has put in their hearts to fulfill his will, and to agree, and give their kingdom unto the beast, until the words of God shall be fulfilled.

18 And the woman which you saw is that great city (Babylon/NWO), *which reigns over the kings* (NWO elite) *of the earth."*

As I mentioned before, the New World Order bloodline "elite" don't care about the harlot minions that work for them. I read there is corporal punishment (black eyes, etc.) if the minions do not accomplish certain tasks. The New World Order "elite" only use the Harlot to get what they want. They have no respect for the Harlot and will just toss her aside when they are done with her, destroying these fools, as it suits their purposes. I think we are seeing that play out before our eyes. I would not want to be in their shoes. So not worth it.

Verse 18 seems so strange – *"the woman* (the Harlot) *actually rules over the kings of the earth."* The Harlot rules over the NWO "elite." As I said before, the Harlot uses their power to run the Media, Hollywood, the Justice system etc., which has protected the NWO "elite." If the Harlot fails, the New World Order elite will fall.

The Harlot has never failed... until now.

We are starting to see the Media Harlot crumble.

Now we are starting to see their crimes exposed.

They failed to control the vote, so we are starting to get true, duly-elected leaders, like our Wonderful President Trump, who are not ruled by the Harlot.

The NWO will throw the Harlot minions under the bus, as they fight to save themselves. We've seen journalists come out with the most ridiculous fake news of Russian collusion and Ukraine-Gate and the Impeachment of President Trump. We've seen them literally make up stories to hype the Covid Pandemic. All the while, covering up the highly documented crimes of the rich and powerful. The Fake News' reputations have tanked.

That has actually helped the people see through the lies. It really is GAME OVER for these creeps! This is going to be quite a show! What a sight! We are getting to see what the Prophets Daniel and Joel and Ezekiel longed to see! We will see Babylon - the City of the New World Order - destroyed! Who is ready to see that?

Meeeeeee!

Just turn the page...

CHAPTER 20
BABYLON IS FALLEN

Now that we have come this far in the study of Revelation, and now that we have come this far, and we understand something of the depth of the depravity of the worldwide cabal, Revelation Chapter 18 will be a piece of cake with icing. Guess what happens in this chapter.

John tells us about the Fall of Babylon!

Hurray!

(Just one question.)

What is Babylon again? LOL!

Just in case you're just trying to get used to the Revelation lingo, here's a reminder: Babylon is not a physical city or nation.

BABYLON is the entire group/cabal that conspired together to enslave and destroy humanity, including the Harlot and the False Prophet. Their leaders are the evil bloodlines. And their commander is satan himself.

Got it?

Their rival is us, symbolically the city of Jerusalem! Translated CITY OF PEACE – which symbolically represents the city, or group of people, lead by the true LORD of the earth – Christ the King.

OK.

So now that we've got that, just one more thing.

Remember that the Book of Revelation is NOT CHRONOLOGICAL. In this section, John is focusing specifically on the Fall of Babylon... (but we will still hear more about Babylon's Fall in later chapters.)

So let's get the popcorn and enjoy the NWO's Destruction!

In this chapter, all those who have gotten rich and powerful due to this evil Beast system will mourn. (We are actually starting to see that. BTW, today's news was about the College Bribery scandal, which exposed many of the Hollyweird "elites." We will have to put a chocolate on their prison cot, to make sure they enjoy their stay.)

One by one, they lose power.

One by one, the old Guard is being dismantled.

One by one, the leaders are dying, being publicly humiliated, and convicted.

This is just the beginning.

Revelation 18

1 "And after these things I saw another angel come down from heaven, having great power; and the earth was lit with his glory.

*2 And he cried mightily with a strong voice, saying, **Babylon the great is fallen, is fallen,** and is become the **habitation of devils,** and the hold of every foul spirit, and a cage of every unclean and hateful bird.*

3 For all nations have drunk of the wine of the wrath of her fornication, and the kings of the earth have committed fornication with her, and the merchants of the earth have grown rich through the abundance of her delicacies.

4 And I heard another voice from heaven, saying, Come out of her, my people, that you be not partakers of her sins, and that you receive not of her plagues.

*5 For her sins have reached unto heaven, and **God hath remembered her iniquities.***

*6 Reward her even as she rewarded you, and **double unto her double according to her works: in the cup which she hath filled fill to her double."***

Here we have yet another angel message! This angel will have great power, and light the earth with his glory! Well that will have to be a very bright star to light the earth!! Which are the brightest stars?

Venus. Jupiter. Saturn.

What if this bright light is actually two of these stars joined together?

Naaaah... that hardly ever happens. Except.

Except...

The year 2020 is epic in the takedown of the worldwide mafia cabal. Even the heavens are announcing the crowning of Christ as King of the World!

On December 21, 2020, just before Christmas, Jupiter overtakes Saturn, symbolizing Jesus obliterating satan's power on earth! In the picture below, Jupiter is on top of Saturn... this is a very, very rare event. What a bright light in the sky that will be! I bet it's the angel message of Revelation 18!

This angel has the wonderful message that those who committed these horrific crimes against humanity, will get the SAME punishment they meted out on the innocent, only DOUBLE!

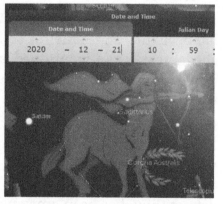

On that same day, December 21, 2020, a comet (C/2017 E1 Borisov) that I call the Christmas Comet, does something very unusual. This comet has always done very small loops on its path through the sky. But it charted a very different path during the Feast of Trumpets, October 2016! This comet started in Leo and shot all the way through the sky to Orion by September 2017, around the time of the Sign of the Son of Man!

At that point it creates a loop... and then a second loop, and then a third loop, crowning Orion (our LORD Jesus) as the King of the World! (See my FreedomForce.LIVE social media link for my video titled Christmas 2020 Comet Crowns Orion - Prince of Peace (December 17, 2017)

HOW AMAZING IS THAT?!!

Who is ready for Jesus to be crowned King of the World?! MEEEEEEEEEE!!

> 7 "How much she has **glorified herself**, and **lived deliciously**, so much torment and sorrow give her: for she said in her heart, I sit a **queen**, and am no widow, and shall see no sorrow."

Their sense of entitlement is noxious.

> 8 "Therefore shall her plagues come **in one day, death, and mourning, and famine**; and she shall be **utterly burned** with fire: for strong is the Lord God who judges her."

How the mighty are falling. Must be tough, after living in the lap of luxury and fame for so long, with impunity. I will not shed a tear. As I mentioned earlier, Queen Elizabeth was just proven to be a fake, and has fled to Windsor Castle. Nope, no tears.

In light of thousands of years, actually the take-down of the New World Order has been amazingly quick. (For those of us who have been fighting hard, each day has been fierce and excruciating. We have waited for justice for so long!) But the dismantling, has been amazingly a single day, in view of all of time since the fall of Adam and the enemy's takeover of the world.

> 9 "And the kings of the earth, who have committed fornication and lived deliciously with her, shall bewail her, and lament for her, when they shall see the smoke of her burning,
>
> 10 Standing afar off for the fear of her torment, saying, Alas, alas that great city Babylon, that mighty city! **for in one hour is your judgment come**.
>
> 11 And the merchants of the earth shall weep and mourn over her; for

no man buys their merchandise any more:

12 The merchandise of gold, and silver, and precious stones, and of pearls, and fine linen, and purple, and silk, and scarlet, and all thyine wood, and all manner vessels of ivory, and all manner vessels of most precious wood, and of brass, and iron, and marble,

*13 And cinnamon, and perfumes, and ointments, and frankincense, and wine, and oil, and fine flour, and wheat, and beasts, and sheep, and horses, and chariots, and **slaves, and souls of men.***

*14 And the fruits that thy soul lusted after are departed from thee, and **all things which were dainty and goodly are departed from you**, and you shall find them no more at all."*

No more easy money-cutting deals to screw the people!

No more cushy government jobs for fake Aunty Suzy!

No more government contracts for a bridge to nowhere!

No more drug and human trafficking blood money!

No more pallets of Two Billion in cash flown to Iran!

No more screwing with our Stock Market!

No more making a killing on killing us with wars and disease!

No more selling our Uranium to Rogue Russians!

No more selling our State secrets to the Chinese!

No more $20 Trillion Federal Reserve Debt to enslave us!

No more villas on the Riviera!

No more laughing in our faces!

Bread and Water.

A Pot and a Cot.

If that.

15 "The merchants of these things, which were made rich by her, shall stand afar off for the fear of her torment, weeping and wailing,

*16 And saying, Alas, alas that great city, that was **clothed in fine linen, and purple**, and scarlet, and decked with gold, and precious stones, and pearls!*

17 For in one hour so great riches is come to nothing. And every shipmaster, and all the company in ships, and sailors, and as many as trade by sea, stood afar off,

18 And cried when they saw the smoke of her burning, saying, What city is like unto this great city!

19 And they cast dust on their heads, and cried, weeping and wailing, saying, Alas, alas that great city, wherein were made rich all that had ships in the sea by reason of her costliness! for in one hour is she made desolate."

I just want to yell, "Quit your crying, you fools! You make me sick that you want this evil to continue!"

Did you notice the purple (New World Order color of royalty) and all the fancy wear?

Orange Jumpsuits instead of Fine Linen.

I hope it's scratchy.

And just look at OUR response to the Demise of the New World Order!

20 "Rejoice over her, you in heaven, and you holy apostles and prophets; for God has avenged you on her.

21 And a mighty angel took up a stone like a great millstone, and cast it into the sea, saying, Thus with violence shall that great city Babylon be thrown down, and shall be found no more at all.

22 And the voice of harpers, and musicians, and of pipers, and trumpeters, shall be heard no more at all in you; and no craftsman, of whatsoever craft he be, shall be found any more in you; and the sound of a millstone shall be heard no more at all in you;

23 And the light of a candle shall shine no more at all in you; and the voice of the bridegroom and of the bride shall be heard no more at all in you: for thy merchants were the great men of the earth; for by thy sorceries were all nations deceived.

24 And in her was found the blood of prophets, and of saints, and of all that were slain upon the earth."

It's ALL getting shut down. Completely. Not even a candle will be left burning in their Evil Empire. Bye!

Did you notice the millstone that was cast into the sea? Reminds us of the verse,

"But whoso shall cause one of these little ones who believe in Me to fall,

it were better for him that a millstone were hung about his neck, and that he were drowned in the depth of the sea." (Matthew 18:6)

They will sink into their place of punishment, never to be seen again. Never to harm another precious one. Ever. And to receive the just punishment due them.

The ones who were made rich because of the New World Order can cry all they want.

We will REJOICE!

AND REJOICE!

AND REJOICE SOME MORE!

God will avenge us for all the damage they have done to our families, our unity, our health, our finances. And the LORD will restore everything, in time. Our lives will be renewed like the eagles. We will have joy that no man can take away!

Let's stop and enjoy God's vengeance on our enemies!

First off! The LORD will make them pay for what they have done. He is angry about what they have done to us, and **they will pay and pay and pay some more**.

For killing our family members with cancer and causing untold suffering, **they will pay!**

For stealing our hard-earned money and making our money practically worthless, **they will pay!**

For causing our families to struggle, and many to separate, due to their incessant deception, **they will pay!**

For stealing our privacy by spying on us through our phones, laptops, TVs, etc., **they will pay!**

For infiltrating the church and the seminaries with secret society members who deceived the unsuspecting masses, **they will pay!**

For creating AIDS, and Autism, and Clinical Depression, and countless other diseases, **they will pay!**

For poisoning us with GMOs and all the other chemicals in the food, and water, and air, and household products, **they will pay**!

For spraying us with chemicals so we had seizures and migraines and depression and Alzheimer's and countless other maladies, **they will pay**!

For filling our society with wickedness, and cursing, and pornography, and vile movies and music, **they will pay!**

For filling our streets with legal and illegal drugs, that destroyed lives and families, and even caused early deaths, **they will pay!**

For fomenting anarchy in our streets and the breakdown of brotherhood of our nations, **they will pay!**

For ripping apart our families, causing fatherlessness and widespread divorce, **they will pay!**

For allowing criminals to roam free to commit crimes throughout our Country, **they will pay!**

For using schools, and entertainment, and social media propaganda to cause our children to mock God, and not believe in Him, **they will pay!**

For sending our sons and daughters to their deaths in illegal proxy wars, **they will pay!**

For the promotion of abortion, causing the deaths of millions of precious children, **they will pay**!

For the abuse of children by those who named the name of Christ, and for covering up this wickedness, **they will pay!**

For trafficking and torturing children and adults, and all the despicable abominations they committed against them, **they will pay!**

REJOICE EVERYONE! SOON WE WILL SHOUT,

"THE LORD HAS AVENGED US ON OUR ENEMIES!"

CHAPTER 21
ALLELUIA FOREVER

We are seeing the dismantling of their evil empire, day after day, all over the world. What a show! But we are so ready to see the Mass Start Awakening! And the 170,000+ ARRESTS!!! We hear that justice is very close. It would seem so from all the truth being exposed, and from our pea-soup sky filled with chemtrails (geoengineering)! The Deep State is fighting in Full Panic Desperation Mode! Completely disorganized. Kinda funny.

In this Revelation Chapter 19, we stop.

We stop and sing!

We stop and rejoice!

We stop and praise the LORD for rescuing us!

We stop and heave a huge sigh of relief!

We aren't rejoicing alone! We are rejoicing with everyone in Heaven and on Earth. The Great and the Small. Everyone together! Unified in Praise that God Reigns and Defeated the Beast New World Order!

So let's go ahead and do that now.

(It will be good for our blood pressure...)

Revelation 19

*1 "And after these things I heard a great voice of much people in heaven, saying, **Alleluia; Salvation, and glory, and honor, and power, unto the Lord our God:***

2 For true and righteous are his judgments: for he has judged the great Harlot, which did corrupt the earth with her fornication, and has avenged the blood of his servants at her hand.

3 And again they said, **Alleluia and her smoke rose up for ever and ever.**

4 And **the four and twenty elders and the four beasts fell down and worshiped God that sat on the throne, saying, Amen; Alleluia.**

5 And a voice came out of the throne, saying, **Praise our God, all you his servants,** *and you that fear him, both small and great.*

6 And I heard as it were **the voice of a great multitude,** *and as the voice of many waters, and as the voice of mighty thunderings, saying,* **Alleluia: for the Lord God omnipotent reigns.**

7 Let us be glad and rejoice, and give honor to him: for the marriage of the Lamb is come, and his wife has made herself ready.

8 And to her was granted that she should be arrayed in fine linen, clean and white: for the fine linen is the righteousness of saints.

9 And he said unto me, Write, Blessed are they which are called unto the marriage supper of the Lamb. And he said unto me, These are the true sayings of God.

10 And I fell at his feet to worship him. And he said unto me, See you do it not: I am your fellow servant, and of your brethren that have the testimony of Jesus: **worship God:** *for the testimony of Jesus is the spirit of prophecy."*

John gets so excited that He begins to worship the wrong person! We are Praising God… let's always remember that all the rest of us are His servants! We always feel so amazing after we stop and give the LORD praise for who He is and all He has done!

So are you ready for the Victory Dance?

We are READY!!

The world is ready for the Kingdom of Christ on earth! The bride is ready for judgment on the Beast. We are finally awake and ready for the truth to come out and for there to be peace on earth!

PRAISE YOU LORD FOR YOUR FAITHFULNESS AND YOUR POWER TO SAVE US FROM OUR ENEMIES! PRAISE YOU

LORD FOR FORGIVING US THROUGH CHRIST SO WE ARE REDEEMED FROM SATAN'S EVIL KINGDOM, AND WILL ENJOY YOUR GLORIOUS KINGDOM FOREVER AND EVER!

FIRE IN HIS EYES AND A SWORD IN HIS MOUTH!

This chapter brings us to the grand finale in this long, tough Battle of Armageddon. What a powerful visual for us! This is exactly where we are in history... whether the Church is awake to know it or not!

> 11 "And I saw heaven opened, and behold a white horse; and he that sat upon him was called **Faithful and True**, and in righteousness he does judge and make war."

Like a heavenly movie set, the curtains of Heaven are opened and Our Wonderful LORD is revealed! He's riding on a white horse - the Champion of the World! Faithful and True because we can count on Him to never let us down. He will judge righteously and fairly, and make war against the Beast/New World Order. After so long fighting and not gaining any ground, what Joy! What a relief! To see our LORD whom we **KNOW** will defeat our enemies! I might have to go back to the Praise portion of the chapter above and get my Praise on again! Just knowing He **WILL** defeat our enemies makes my heart leap for joy!

Before we continue, I have to say this is **SYMBOLIC LANGUAGE**. Not in regard to our LORD'S power, but in regard to the literal white horse flying down from heaven. I really don't believe it will happen with a physical white horse flying. Yes, yes, I know that is what we have been taught. And yes, yes, I know He is able to do all things. But to be a student of the book of Revelation, we must read the symbolic language as SYMBOLIC. I believe this verse is saying that at just the right moment, symbolically the "clouds" will clear, and our LORD will be revealed. Our Savior here to save us! He will be faithful and true. He will judge in righteousness. And He will destroy the Beast/NWO.

I think I used to have an image of Jesus appearing and zapping the bad guys with lightning bolts... and almost magically the angels would gather people, and Jesus would separate out all the people of the earth, yelling "Sheep to the Right - Goats to the Left!" That was a little simplistic.

But didn't the angels say Jesus would return **in the clouds** just like He left?

That's not exactly what they said.

This is the *Message* version, which I think grasps the meaning of what the angels told the disciples.

> *"These were his last words. As they watched, he was taken up and disappeared in a cloud. They stood there, staring into the empty sky. Suddenly two men appeared—in white robes! They said, "You Galileans!—why do you just stand here looking up at an empty sky? This very Jesus who was taken up from among you to heaven* **will come as certainly—and mysteriously—as he left**." *(Acts 1:11)*

He left in bodily form. In a very unusual way.
He will return in bodily form. In a very unusual way.
Remember, the idiom *"coming on the clouds"* has a symbolic meaning throughout literature It means for someone coming into POWER and AUTHORITY.
This is something to consider and pray about.
If the LORD returns in a different way, I don't want to be like the disciples, standing there looking up in the sky! LOL!

The point is... our LORD appears on the scene just when we need Him most. And make no mistake about it. It is a real war. Not with guns and tanks. But the Beast and False Prophet are not going down without a fight. And their hatred of Jesus will be just the same as it was 2,000 years ago. But this time they WON'T be able to kill Him!

Rejoice that our LORD is the WORLD CHAMPION!

Rejoice that our LORD is FAITHFUL!

Rejoice that our LORD KEEPS HIS PROMISES!

Rejoice that our LORD is A VALIANT WARRIOR!

Rejoice that our LORD WILL DESTROY THE WICKED!

Rejoice that our LORD is THE KING OVER EVERY KING IN HEAVEN AND ON EARTH!

I found a new *interesting nugget.*

Our LORD has five names in this chapter!

His name, <u>Faithful and True</u>, is the first of these five names for our LORD. As we go through the chapter, I will point out His other names.

> 12 *"His eyes were as a flame of fire, and on his head were many crowns; and **he had a name written, that no man knew, but he himself.**"*

Think about this. Jesus might not go by the name Jesus. He has <u>a new name</u> that only He Himself knows. Hmmm... Any ideas what that might be? I feel sure it will be a word commonly used in God's Word.

> 13 *"And he was clothed with a vesture dipped in blood: and his name is called **The Word of God.**"*

He has yet another name, (His third name of this chapter). He tells us this one... <u>the Word of God.</u> The very breath and truth of Almighty God.

This blood on his clothing is NOT His own blood. This is the blood of His and our enemies! Wow! What an image!

> 14 *"And the armies which were in heaven followed him upon white horses, clothed in fine linen, white and clean."*

That's us! We are in that mighty army, my Patriot brothers and sisters! Along with the angels and other believers already in Heaven! We are seated with authority with Him in Heaven (high powerful places), in integrity to wage this righteous war!

> 15 *"And out of his mouth goes a sharp sword, that with it he should smite the nations: and he shall rule them with a rod of iron: and he treads the wine-press of the fierceness and wrath of Almighty God."*

A sharp sword and rod of iron are devastating weapons. Don't expect our LORD Jesus to speak kindly to the New World Order minions. His very words will cut them down! And He will break them down, destroy their authority, and crush them with exposure, prosecution, and sentencing. He won't stop until they drink down all the wrath of Almighty God for their horrific crimes.

> 16 *"And he has on his vesture and on his thigh **a name written, KING of kings, and LORD of lords**."*

Here's another name for our LORD (His fourth name of this chapter) - <u>KING of kings</u> = He rules over kings with governmental power to rule the nations of the world.

And <u>LORD of lords</u> (His fifth name of this chapter) – He rules over every heart and life – as we all surrender our wills to His wise and perfect will. Imagine everyone doing that... what a beautiful world. True, lasting peace on earth.

> 17 *"And I saw an angel standing in the sun; and he cried with a loud voice, saying to all the fowls that fly in the midst of heaven, **Come and gather** yourselves together unto the supper of the great God;*
>
> 18 *That you may eat the flesh of kings, and the flesh of captains, and the flesh of mighty men, and the flesh of horses, and of them that sit on them, and the flesh of all men, both free and bond, both small and great."*

GET READY for a bloodbath of prosecutions! Just like the heavens depict Corvus the bird, feasting on the giant serpent, and Crater, the cup of the wrath of God being poured out!

> 19 *"And I saw the beast, and the kings of the earth, and their armies, gathered together to make war against him that sat on the horse, and against his army.*
>
> 20 *And the beast was taken, and with him the false prophet that*

*worked miracles before him, with which he deceived them that had received the mark of the beast, and them that worshiped his image. **These both were cast alive into a lake of fire burning with brimstone.***"

Notice that the Beast and False Prophet are cast into torment, but NOT those who were deceived into joining the New World Order. The punishment for those at the top of the New World Order, who KNOWINGLY destroyed humanity, is more severe than the punishment for those who were tricked into taking the mark of the beast and following their evil plan. The Beast and False Prophet are cast alive into torment – (sounds like the death penalty, and worse). They will never work their evil magic again!

> 21 "*And the remnant were slain with the sword of him that sat upon the horse, which sword proceeds out of his mouth: and all the fowls were filled with their flesh.*"

The rest will be prosecuted and rot in prison. Doubtful they will ever be able to walk the streets again anyway, after the masses realize what they have done.

The battle is about exposing their fakery and crimes, and then prosecuting them.

As I am writing this, we are just getting started with their exposure and prosecution. Hang on tight! This reminds me of a roller coaster ride we used to take at Opryland. The climb up the hill inched ever so slowly, bit by bit, and finally we reached the precipice! Then all of a sudden, down the track we would careen, twisting and turning on the ride of our lives. Make sure you're strapped in tightly Patriot brothers and sisters! This will truly be the ride of all time! And we have a front row seat! (Thanks!)

Whoever put the chapter breaks in the Bible must have been part of the Deep State! He stopped right in the middle of our moment of Victory!

Chapter 19 ended with:

> *"And the remnant were slain with the sword of him that sat upon the horse, which sword proceeds out of his mouth: and all the fowls were filled with their flesh."*

What happens next?! Tell me! Tell me!

Revelation 20
> 1 *"And I saw an angel come down from heaven, having the key of the bottomless pit and a great chain in his hand*
> 2 *And he laid hold on the dragon, that old serpent, which is the devil, and satan, and **bound him a thousand years**."*

Not only are the Beast and the False Prophet gone and in the abyss...

but so is the Devil!!

For 1,000 years!

Wrap your head around this glorious thought...

Satan bound for 1,000 years!!!

1,000 years!!!

No satan!!!

No deception!!!

Up off our throats!!!

Did I say 1,000 years??!!!

YAHOOOOO!

So how could that happen, exactly? Satan works through humans, as they allow the demons to use them. But with satan's minions gone... he's gone too! His power to destroy the world is squashed! Yahoo!

We are part of this Great Battle under the leadership of President Donald J. Trump, that is exposing and defeating the Beast New World Order. No doubt about it. They will be cast out.

Out!

Out!

OUT!

3 "And cast him into the bottomless pit, shut him up, and set a seal upon him, that he should deceive the nations no more, til the thousand years should be fulfilled: after that he must be loosed a little season."

Oh dear. I love the part about sealing satan up in the bottomless pit. For 1,000 years! But loosing him for a little season... that part I do NOT love.

So why?

Why?

WHY??!!!

Let's just not talk about it. Let's pretend that's not in there... for now... we will talk about that in the chapter on the FINAL BATTLE - the Gog and Magog Battle. But the LORD wants us to know from the very outset, that the Millennial Kingdom is NOT Heaven on earth... not yet. The Millennial Reign is soooo much more wonderful than anything we have ever experienced! But it's not the New Heaven and the New Earth. As wonderful as the Millennial Kingdom on earth will be, the New Heaven and the New Earth are EVEN BETTER! That's the eternal cherry on top! But that's AFTER the Battle of Gog and Magog. We will talk about that two chapters from now.

Ok... Next. Deep Breath.

There is a verse that is super strange. I wonder if I should just skip it.

Do y'all want me to skip it?

Ok... I will just skip it.

Because it's really strange.

What?

You want me to just throw my idea out there?

Really?

You're sure now?

Promise not to laugh?

Ok... but remember you promised!

Read this verse...

> 4 "And I saw thrones, and they sat upon them, and judgment was given unto them."

That verse is simple enough. We will rule with Christ on this earth! We will have good leaders who love the LORD and serve people and make wise decisions in every area, from corporations to media to government to education to entertainment... etc., all over the world!

It took 2,000 years to go into all the world and make disciples, just as Jesus commanded. Now we have Christ-followers trained up to take these positions and rule with and for Christ! That's great news! That's the easy part of this verse.

Read on.

> "and I saw the souls of them that were beheaded for the witness of Jesus, and for the word of God, and which had not worshiped the beast, neither his image, neither had received his mark upon their foreheads, or in their hands; and **they lived and reigned with Christ a thousand years**."

What?!!

They Lived?!

They LIVED!!

And **REIGNED** with Him 1,000 years?!

I know I've told you some amazing promises in this book, but that right there, my friends, is...

AMAAAAAAA-ZING!!!

Ok... on the face of the verse it says basically this:

Good guys tried to fight the bad guys.

They got killed for it. *(they were beheaded)*

Think Andrew Breitbart.   Think JFK.

They didn't join with the NWO Beast.

Instead they fought the NWO Beast.

They fought the NWO Beast with the minds/words (foreheads) and their actions (hands).

And then.

Did you read the rest of the verse?

It says **THEY LIVED.**

I'm not going to speculate on how the LORD will do this.

But somehow, it appears from this verse, those who have proven themselves as faithful Patriots, will return to earth for an encore performance!

Do you realize how wild that sounds?

They will rule with Christ for the entire 1,000 years!

However the LORD does it, imagine if these PROVEN PATRIOTS like JFK were back!

How helpful would that be to making sure no one plays with demonic fire?!

I told you that verse was strange! LOL! But no stranger than our confidence that Christ was raised from the dead! If He can raise Himself from the dead, He can certainly raise JFK!

> 5 "But the rest of the dead lived not again until the thousand years were finished. This is the first resurrection.
>
> 6 Blessed and holy is he that has part in the first resurrection: on such the second death hath no power, but they shall be priests of God and of

Christ, and shall reign with him a thousand years."

These faithful soldiers - like JFK - get a special reward. They get their resurrected new bodies early. They get to reign with Christ for the 1,000 years!

They can't be killed.

Bullet-proof.

Drown-proof.

Poison-proof.

Germ-proof.

Evil-proof.

Like Super Heroes!

These verses might be symbolic, but I can't see how.

Before we continue with the rest of Revelation, we need to take a break and enjoy the Millennial Reign for about 1,000 years! Let's bask in all the wonderful things the LORD has planned for us!

CHAPTER 22
THE MARVELOUS MILLENNIAL REIGN OF CHRIST ON EARTH

Welcome to the Millennial Reign of Christ on earth. Settle in. Get comfy. We're going to enjoy our new lives for 1,000 years! I love how he quotes,

"For I know the plans I have for you", declares the LORD, "plans to prosper you and not to harm you, to give you hope and a future." (Jeremiah 29:11)

Want to know what some of those plans are? It seems like we spend so much time talking about all the troubles, we forget to focus on the Glorious, Bright, Beautiful Future the LORD has planned for us!

Health, Wealth, Peace, Unity

Buckle up! This is going to be AMAZING! These promises are all throughout God's Word - I will point out a few here:

Excerpts from Isaiah 60

1 "Arise, shine; for your light is come, and the glory of the Lord is risen upon you.

2...the Lord shall arise upon you, and his glory shall be seen upon you.

3 And the Gentiles shall come to your light **(evildoers will recognize you're blessed of God)**, *and kings to the **brightness of your radiance.***

*4 Lift up your eyes and look and see: they all **gather themselves together and are coming home! Your sons shall come from far, and your daughters will be carried home.***

*5 Then **your eyes will sparkle, and your heart shall fill with joy;** because the **abundance of goods shall be brought to you, your wealth will return to you.***

*6 ...they shall **bring offerings and worship the Lord.***

*7...they shall come up with acceptance on mine altar, and I **will glorify the house of my glory.***

*9... **they will bring your sons from far, their silver and their gold with them,** unto the name of the Lord your God, and to the Holy One of Israel, because he has glorified you.*

*10 **Foreigners will rebuild your towns.***

*14 The sons also of them that afflicted you **shall come bowing down to you;** and all they that despised you shall bow themselves down at the soles of your feet; and **they shall call you; God's People - The City of the Lord,** The Zion of the Holy One of Israel.*

*15 Whereas you had been forsaken and hated, so that no man went through you, I **will make you an eternal excellency, a joy of many generations.***

*16 **Kings will meet your every need:** and you will know that I **the Lord am your Savior and your Redeemer.***

*17 **Instead of brass you will have gold,** and instead of iron you will have silver, and instead of wood brass, and instead of stones iron: I will also make **peace your ruler,** and **righteousness your leader.***

*18 **Violence shall no more be heard in your land, no more destruction within your borders;** but you shall call your walls Salvation, and your gates Praise."*

And more...

Isaiah 11:9 **NO MORE HARM OR DESTRUCTION AT ALL**

*"They will not hurt or destroy in all My holy mountain, For the earth will be **full of the knowledge of the LORD** as the waters fill the sea."*

Isaiah 11:4 **JUSTICE**

*"But with **righteousness He will judge the poor,** And decide with fairness for the afflicted of the earth; And He will strike the earth with the rod of His mouth, And with the breath of His lips He will slay the wicked."*

Habakkuk 2:14 **KNOWLEDGE OF THE LORD EVERYWHERE!**

"For the earth will be filled with the knowledge of the glory of the LORD, as the waters fill the sea."

Isaiah 2:2-4 **TRUE FAITH IN CHRIST EVERYWHERE!**

"Now it will come about that in the last days, the mountain of the house of the LORD will be established as the chief of the mountains, and will be raised above the hills; and all the nations will stream to it."

Isaiah 11:6 **NO FEAR OF DANGER**

"And the wolf will dwell with the lamb, and the leopard will lie down with the young goat, and the calf and the young lion and the fatling together; and a little boy will lead them."

Isaiah 65:20 **LIFE EXTENSION**

"No longer will there be in it an infant who lives but a few days, or an old man who does not live out his days; for the youth will die at the age of one hundred, the one who does not reach the age of one hundred will be thought unfortunate."

Check out the "Super Jubilee-All Debts Paid" video on our Freedom Force.LIVE social media link. This video explains possibly how some of these promises will be fulfilled. Imagine all your income taxes and interest returned to you, and our national debt wiped out! All this money was stolen from us by the cabal! WOWEE! Buckle up!

This sounds too good to be true!

But this is the Word of God.

These are His own promises to us.

And somehow, some way, it **WILL** HAPPEN.

CHAPTER 23
JUDGMENT DAY
GOG & MAGOG BATTLE
THE BOTTOMLESS PIT

Have you heard of the Gog and Magog Battle? Most people I talk to don't know anything about this battle! All "End Times" attention is on the Armageddon Battle. If people focus on the Gog and Magog Battle, most of the "End Times" deceptions crumble!

The Gog and Magog Battle is **AFTER** the 1,000 years of Christ's Reign on earth in the Millennial Kingdom. This is the final battle before the New Heaven, the New Earth, and our New Bodies... EVERYTHING WILL BE INCORRUPTIBLE! It will be like the Garden of Eden, but better! Let's see what happens in this Gog and Magog Battle.

Revelation 20

> 7 *"And when the thousand years are expired* (**after 1,000 years of peace in Christ's Millennial Reign**), *satan shall be loosed out of his prison,*
>
> 8 *And shall go out to deceive the nations which are in the four quarters of the earth, Gog, and Magog, to gather them together to battle: the number of whom is as the sand of the sea."*

Remember how I said I didn't want to talk about Revelation 20:3 before? This verse right here:

> 3 *"And cast him into the bottomless pit, shut him up, and set a seal upon him, that he should deceive the nations no more, til the thousand years should be fulfilled:* ***after that he must be loosed a little season."***

Well, now it's time to talk about it. Why is satan loosed after the 1,000 year Millennial Reign of Christ on earth?

Why?

Why?

WHY????

To answer that, here is a helpful section from Matthew 12 about demonic spirits. Scripture answers many of our questions if we look carefully. We shouldn't rely on human reasoning without the guidance of God's Word.

> *"When the unclean spirit is gone out of a man, he walks through dry places, seeking rest, and finds none. Then he said, I will return into my house from where I came out; and when he is come, he finds it empty, swept, and garnished.*
>
> *Then he goes, and takes with himself seven other spirits more wicked than himself, and they enter in and dwell there: and the last state of that man is worse than the first. Even so shall it be also unto this wicked generation."* (Matthew 12)

Do you get it? Demonic spirits operate through a host. A human. That is how they do evil on the earth. THAT is how the Beast New World Order has operated, done so much evil, gained so much wealth, all the while keeping us in the dark about what they were doing. Straight up satanic power as they are *joined* with - *one with* - humans... <u>literally demons dwelling in humans</u>. These are Nephalim - the ones who are indwelt by demons.

AWAKE YET?

That is all being exposed and will be defeated, as one by one these criminals are prosecuted and eliminated!

The exposure of the Beast's and False Prophet's horrific crimes against humanity, and their coming terrifying prosecution and demise will strike fear in humanity from ever toying with demonic spirits again. Safeguards such as memorials, corrected textbooks, videos of trials and executions, etc., will be established. Everyone will realize that all the hell we have been through was due to the NWO being under demonic control. That fact alone will likely carry us peacefully into the 1,000 years of Christ's reign on earth.

What the entire earth is soon to witness, is not just a political movement that will reverse in a future political cycle. This is a change that will transform the whole world to its very core. Once the truth comes out, and we are free from all the effects of their crimes and tyranny, there will be tremendous caution and resolve to never, Never, NEVER allow this Ever Again!

But.

But.

Human nature has the tendency to forget. To become lax. It's so hard for me to imagine this world without the enemy, I can't begin to imagine 1,000 years without him causing mayhem! Buuuuut, even without demonic forces, people will still have their selfishness and foolishness to deal with, and the worldly temptations... so I think there will still be a few issues, knowing what I know about human nature. So, those who really are dead-set on rebelling against the LORD, will try to bring others down with them. Even with the life extension that the Bible talks about us having during the 1,000 year Millennial Reign, there might not be enough old timers to warn the next Millennials of the dangers of toying with the demonic. That's when the world will be reminded just how dark the dark side is.

The enemy will launch an attack on God's people. My guess is that somehow the enemy will find a way to re-light this fire from the pits of hell, allowing the demons to work on earth again. If I tried to describe it, it would probably sound like a rerun of a Star Trek episode! Maybe it will be some futuristic supercomputer AI. Maybe something Matrix-y. I hate to talk about it, but I have to, because the LORD talked about it.

So here's what happens in the Gog and Magog Battle:

9 *"And they went up on the breadth of the earth, and compassed the camp of the saints about, and the beloved city: and **fire came down from God out of heaven, and devoured them.**"*

Satan is back at his evil tricks, and it appears he has the entire world in a spiritual head-lock.   But God.   It's always BUT GOD. (Search the Bible for "But God" verses - He is continually rescuing us!)   At the Gog and Magog battle, God does another miracle to rescue humanity. He zaps the demons into oblivion! Sounds so much like the time fire came down from heaven on the altar, when Elijah had the showdown with Jezebel's Baal worshipers. Zaaaaaappppp!

10 *"And the devil that deceived them was cast into the lake of fire and brimstone, where the beast and the false prophet are, and shall be tormented day and night for ever and ever."*

Satan's power will be broken FOREVER!

Humanity will be freed FOREVER!

The evil ones will be locked out and tormented FOREVER! Then we will have eternal Heaven on Earth!

11 *"And I saw a great white throne, and him that sat on it, from whose face the earth and the heaven fled away; and there was found no place for them.*

12 *And I saw the dead, small and great, stand before God; and the **books were opened:** and another book was opened, which is **the book of life**: and the dead were judged out of those things which were written in the books, according to their works."*

So who are these "DEAD"? Those Dead to God. Dead spiritually. No connection with God on a personal level.

"And you has he quickened (made alive to God), *who were dead in trespasses and sins."* (Ephesians 2:1)

"Likewise reckon yourselves to be dead indeed to sin, but alive to God through Jesus Christ our Lord." (Romans 6:11)

Instead of being alive in fellowship with God, these people are

DEAD to God. These DEAD will be judged by their works - every thought, every word, every action. Oh dear.

No one can *stand* under that judgment.

Talk about Hammer Time!

PRAISE the LORD that we who have faith in Christ stand BLAMELESS, PERFECT in God's sight!

> *"He made Him who knew no sin to be sin for us **that we might become the righteousness of God in Him**."* (2nd Corinthians 5:21)

If you have not turned from sin and received forgiveness and new life as a free gift from the LORD Jesus Christ, put this book down and do it now. You MUST be right with Him to stand blameless before God.

Did you do it?

Seriously.

DO IT NOW.

LORD, I know only Your blood shed on the cross can forgive my sin and give me power to walk in Your ways. I turn from everything that opposes Your holy will and put my trust in You to make me stand blameless on the Day of Judgment. Dwell within me from this moment forward. Thank You LORD for Your Great Love for me. In Jesus' name I pray, Amen

OK.   Now we can go on.

In this Great White Throne Judgment, there are two sets of books.

One set is the Book of Life. That is the list of everyone who has truly repented and has true living faith in Christ. Anyone whose name is not written in this Book of Life will be cast into the Lake of Fire. (verse 15)

The other set is the Book of Works. Every Thought. Every Word. Every Action. Of Every Person. For All Time. The DEAD are judged out of this Book of Works.

At the end of this Great White Throne Judgment, it will be OBVIOUS to everyone that the LORD gave each and every person on earth the knowledge and the opportunity to repent and receive forgiveness, but some flatly refused.

> 13 "And the sea gave up the dead which were in it; and death and hell delivered up the dead which were in them: and they were judged every man according to their works.
>
> 14 And death and hell were cast into the lake of fire. This is the second death.
>
> 15 And whosoever was not found written in the book of life was cast into the lake of fire."

This is when human spirits are re-joined with their bodies. The DEAD do not get resurrected new bodies. They are rejoined with their dead bodies. Re-joined Forever. Putrefying Stench. Sounds like a Second Death to me. Cast into hell.

That's what they wanted - to exist apart from God.

They get their wish.

Forgiveness is free.

But forgiveness is not forced on anyone.

The LORD will execute His final judgment on the rebels, and that will be the end of rebellion. Done.

And then there will be no more death. Ever.

Everyone remaining will be judged and rewarded. At that point, death will be no more... because all true Christ followers will have their resurrected body, just like Jesus already has!

> "For **we must all appear** before the judgment seat of Christ; that every one may receive the things done in his body, according to that he has done, whether it be good or bad." (2nd Corinthians 5:10)

> "**Every man's work shall be made manifest to all**: for the day shall

declare it, because it shall be revealed by fire; and the fire shall try every man's work of what sort it is. If any man's work abide which he has built upon, he shall receive a reward. If any man's work shall be burned, he shall suffer loss: but he himself shall be saved; yet so as by fire." (1st Corinthians 3:13-15)

Believers will receive rewards for their faithfulness. Faithless fake works will be burned up.

"Then comes the end, when he shall have delivered up the kingdom to God, even the Father; when he shall have put down all rule and all authority and power. For he must reign, til he ha put all enemies under his feet. The last enemy that shal be destroyed is death." (1st Corinthians 15:23-25)

Christ is going to deliver the Kingdom to the Father. But that won't happen until Christ defeats every enemy, including death.

As Peter said, "But the (judgment) *day of the LORD will come like a thief. The heavens will disappear with a roar, the elements will be dissolved in the fire, and the earth and its works will not be found. Since everything will be dissolved in this way, what kind of people ought you to be?"* (2nd Peter 3:10)

The old worn-out heaven and earth will dissolve to make way for the New Heaven and New Earth! This is going to happen, and there is nothing anyone can do to thwart God's plan. The only thing for us to do, is to humble ourselves and be a part of what He is doing!

WOW! WHAT AN AMAZING PLAN!

CHAPTER 24
UNSPEAKABLE JOY!

Here is the beautiful account of the New Heaven and New Earth coming down from heaven... sparkling and radiant, with golden streets, and pearly gates.

Revelation 21

1 "And I saw a new heaven and a new earth: for the first heaven and the first earth were passed away; and there was no more sea.

2 And I John saw the holy city, new Jerusalem, coming down from God out of heaven, prepared as a bride adorned for her husband.

3 And I heard a great voice out of heaven saying, Behold, the tabernacle of God is with men, and he will dwell with them, and they shall be his people, and God himself shall be with them, and be their God.

*4 And **God shall wipe away all tears from their eyes; and there shall be no more death, neither sorrow, nor crying, neither shall there be any more pain: for the former things are passed away.***

5 And he that sat upon the throne said, Behold, I make all things new. And he said to me, Write: for these words are true and faithful.

6 And he said unto me, It is done. I am Alpha and Omega, the beginning and the end. I will give unto him that is thirsty of the fountain of the water of life freely.

7 He that overcomes shall inherit all things; and I will be his God, and he shall be my son.

8 But the fearful, and unbelieving, and the abominable, and murderers, and whoremongers, and sorcerers, and idolaters, and all liars, shall have their part in the lake which burns with fire and brimstone: which is the second death.

9 And there came unto me one of the seven angels which had the seven vials full of the seven last plagues, and talked with me, saying, Come hither, I will show you the bride, the Lamb's wife.

10 And he carried me away in the spirit to a great and high mountain, and showed me that great city, the holy Jerusalem, descending out of heaven from God,

11 Having the glory of God: and her light was like unto a stone most precious, even like a jasper stone, clear as crystal;

12 And had a wall great and high, and had twelve gates, and at the gates twelve angels, and names written thereon, which are the names of the twelve tribes of the children of Israel:

13 On the east three gates; on the north three gates; on the south three gates; and on the west three gates.

14 And the wall of the city had twelve foundations, and in them the names of the twelve apostles of the Lamb.

15 And he that talked with me had a golden reed to measure the city, and the gates thereof, and the wall thereof.

16 And the city lies foursquare, and the length is as large as the breadth: and he measured the city with the reed, twelve thousand furlongs. The length and the breadth and the height of it are equal.

17 And he measured the wall thereof, a hundred and forty and four cubits, according to the measure of a man, that is, of the angel.

18 And the building of the wall of it was of jasper: and the city was pure gold, like unto clear glass.

19 And the foundations of the wall of the city were garnished with all manner of precious stones. The first foundation was jasper; the second, sapphire; the third, a chalcedony; the fourth, an emerald;

20 The fifth, sardonyx; the sixth, sardius; the seventh, chrysolyte; the eighth, beryl; the ninth, a topaz; the tenth, a chrysoprasus; the eleventh, a jacinth; the twelfth, an amethyst.

21 And the twelve gates were twelve pearls: every several gate was of one pearl: and the street of the city was pure gold, as it were transparent glass.

22 And I saw no temple therein: for the Lord God Almighty and the Lamb are the temple of it.

23 And the city had no need of the sun, neither of the moon, to shine in it: for the glory of God did lighten it, and the Lamb is the light thereof.

24 And the nations of them which are saved shall walk in the light of it: and the kings of the earth do bring their glory and honor into it.

25 And the gates of it shall not be shut at all by day: for there shall be no night there.

26 And they shall bring the glory and honor of the nations into it.

27 And there shall in no wise enter into it any thing that defiles, neither whatsoever work abomination, or makes a lie: but they which are written in the Lamb's book of life."

Out with the Old!

In with the New!

New Bodies!

New Earth!

New Heaven!

Never to decay or get worn out!

So, think with me... during the Millennial Reign, we will still have sin in the world, even though it will be in much better condition, without disasters, deception, and the devil, beast and false prophet, etc.

But there's more! After the Gog and Magog battle, the LORD will give us a brand spankin' new everything! And best of all, God Himself will dwell with us. Reminiscent of the Garden of Eden, except that now those in the New Heaven and New Earth know what Adam and Eve never could have known. Namely, the horrible devastating consequences of sin. And that the LORD loved them so much he would suffer and die in their place, so that they could live together happily ever after.

No sorrow or sadness.

No evil or deception.

No lack or pain.

No fear or worry.

No thirst or hunger.

Only pure unmitigated joy and love and peace and fellowship.

Beautiful beyond words.

Knowing even as we are known.

Seeing our LORD face to face. God dwelling with His people forever, as it should have been from the very beginning. But even better.

That is the understanding I have so far. I am continually asking for more revelation on the Book of Revelation. I'm getting more puzzle pieces daily, as the LORD promised that at the end, knowledge would increase.

I am very thankful the LORD put so much in His Word for us, so we wouldn't be alarmed when we see these things happening. So thankful that He knows the end from the beginning! So thankful that He has the whole world, and us, safely in His hands. And that maybe, if we seek Him and His Word, we can be like the wise men, and know the signs of His appearing!

So I will end, just like the Revelation ends, "Come Quickly, LORD Jesus! HURRY!!!" I, for one, cannot wait!!

HEAVENLY STAR SIGNS IN REVELATION

T he Book of Revelation is chock-full of heavenly wonders - star signs the LORD placed in the sky to let us know what He is doing on the earth. The LORD told us in Genesis 1:14 that He "created the sun, moon, and stars for SIGNS, seasons, days and years." Sadly, the enemy hid most of this information from us. I have been able to research and piece together the meanings of the constellations, based on the names of the stars. And in my research I have been able to decode the heavenly signs the LORD gave us in Revelation to help us know that this is the Great Day of the LORD!

The heavens actually do declare the glory of God!

Enjoy!

Revelation 10 - The Great Awakening Sign

Mercury does a 79-day loop in Aquarius signaling the Great Awakening of humanity (January - April 2020)
(details in Chapter 11)

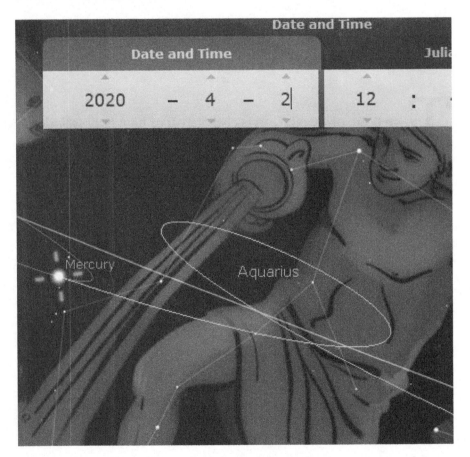

Revelation 12 - The Sign of the Son of Man

This sign began during the Feast of Trumpets, October 2, 2016, and created the Revelation 12 sign on September 23, 2017. This sign has four phases. (Chapter 13)

BIRTH PHASE
Trump Election & Q posts (Nov 10, '16 – Aug 31,'17)
JUDGMENT PHASE
Exposure & Indictments (Dec 25, '17 – Oct 15, '18)
WRESTLING PHASE
NWO Power Removed (Jan 10, 2019 – Oct 31, 2019)
DESTRUCTION PHASE
Prosecutions Begin (Feb 23, 2020 – Dec 25, 2020)

Jupiter's loop in Virgo. (Phase 1 - Birth Phase.)

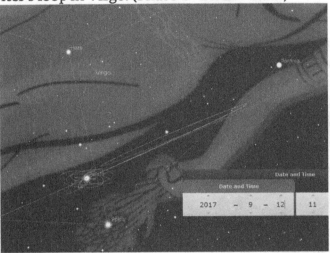

Jupiter's loop through Libra. (Phase 2-Judgment Phase)

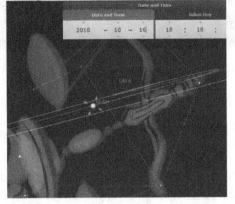

Jupiter's zigzag sine wave path through Ophiuchus.
(Phase 3 - Wrestling Phase)

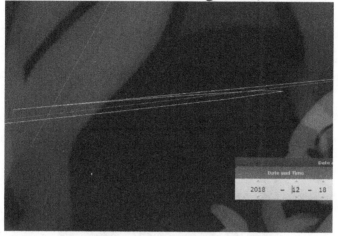

Jupiter's sine wave through Sagittarius.
(Phase 4 - Destruction)

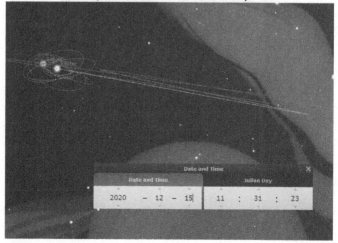

Revelation 14 - The Three Angel Messengers
Messenger # 1 - Mercury in Libra "Judgment has Come"

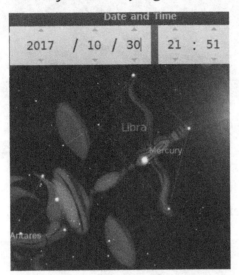

Messenger # 2 - Venus in Scorpio "Babylon is Fallen"

Messenger # 3 - Mars in Ophiuchus "Come Out Now"

Revelation 15 - The Sign of God's Wrath

Venus, symbolizing the love of God, is currently doing a zigzag sine wave through Taurus, on a rampage to destroy the evil New World Order. (see Chapter 17)

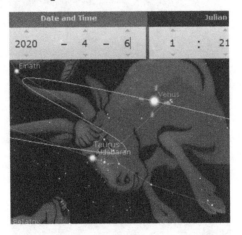

Revelation 18 - The Sign "Babylon is Fallen."

Jupiter (Christ) and Saturn (satan) both loop in Sagittarius. Jupiter overtakes Saturn on December 21, 2020, signaling the end of Babylon! (see Chapter 20)

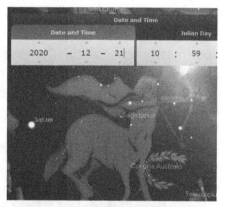

During Christmas 2020, a comet (c/2017 E Borisov) crowns Orion as King of the world! Orion symbolizes Jesus as the Great Hunter/Champion. (Chapter 20)

On March 2, 2023 Venus and Jupiter conjoined, as if to indicate a turning point in the Battle of Armageddon. After that, the exposure of the criminals took a decided turn. The US involvement in the war in Ukraine; the Wuhan lab leak; the Big Pharma gain of function exposure; the classified documents scandal; the Congressional investigations of Big Tech and the FBI; the BRICS nations trading; the East Palestine train derailment disaster ignored by the government; the crash of the banking cartel.

Babylon is falling.

HELPFUL HINTS

1,260 DAYS

1,260 days =3 ½ years = 42 months = Time, Times, and Half a Time = Battle between Good and Evil

What is the significance?

I believe these clues point us to the battle we must wage against evil in this world.

DAWNING OF THE AGE OF AQUARIUS

For those of us from the 70's, you might remember the hit song, "This is the Dawning of the Age of Aquarius." I sang it and never knew what it meant! Well, remember I told you about the giant clock in the sky - the Mazzaroth, made up of all those beautiful constellations that tell God's story to all creation? Since Jesus' time, we have been in the Age of Pisces... the two fish... like Fishers of Men gathering fish for 2,000 years. Get it?

In our day, we are entering the Age of Aquarius. What's that, you say? Well, I'm so glad you asked because I was going to tell you anyway. Aquarius is a constellation depicting a man pouring water out of a huge pitcher! Like the Holy Spirit being poured out on all flesh, as prophesied in Joel 2:28. When everyone will know the LORD! When the young will prophesy, and the old will dream dreams, and the youth will have visions. When knowledge will increase, and people will wake up all over the world to cast out evil, and rule this world in peace. That is happening now, because the Spirit of God is being poured out on all flesh!

For more on Biblical Astronomy and what each constellation represents, check the "Signs in the Sun, Moon, and Stars" playlist on the FreedomForce.LIVE social media link.

ISRAEL

And while we are at it, let's make sure we are all on the same page when we read a verse about Israelites or Jews or Hebrews. When you read the word Israelite or Jew or Hebrew, sometimes the context is about the physical lineage, but most times it is talking about "God's family." The word Israel includes believers from the physical lineage of the "lost tribes" of Israel that have been scattered worldwide. (See "Missing Links Discovered in Assyrian Tablets" by E. Raymond Capt for where the lost tribes are now.) And the names Israel and Jew many times include believers by "adoption" too!

Historically, Israelites are the 10 northern tribes, the Jews are the two southern tribes, and Hebrews are Abraham's seed. Depending on the context, the name Jew could mean:

- a person with the physical lineage of Judah, or

- fake Jews (some are actually Edomites from Esau), or

- Messianic Jews (Judahite believers in Christ), or

- simply Jews in a general sense, encompassing all of God's people.

You see the subject is complex! Believers from every nation are what the Bible calls True Israelites and True Jews. This is very important. The enemy has used this subject to cause unbelievable confusion. Yes, there are differences because of ethnicity. But the most important distinction, especially for this book, is to see God's promises to His entire family, whether by blood lineage or by "adoption."

"Those who are of faith, are sons of Abraham." (Galatians 3:7)

"For he is not a Jew, which is one outwardly; neither is that circumcision, which is outward in the flesh: But he is a Jew, which is one inwardly; and circumcision is that of the heart, in the spirit, and not in

the letter; whose praise is not of men, but of God." (Romans 2:28-29)

16 "Now to Abraham and his seed were the promises made. He said not, And to seeds, as of many; but as of one, And to your seed, which is Christ.

17 And this I say, that the covenant, that was confirmed before God in Christ, the law, which was four hundred and thirty years after, cannot disannul, that it should make the promise of none effect.

18 For if the inheritance be of the law, it is no more of promise: but God gave it to Abraham by promise.

19 What is the purpose of the law? It was added because of transgressions, till the seed should come to whom the promise was made; and it was ordained by angels in the hand of a mediator.

20 Now a mediator is not a mediator of one, but God is one.

21 Is the law then against the promises of God? God forbid: for if there had been a law given which could have given life, verily righteousness should have been by the law.

22 But the Scripture has concluded all under sin, that the promise by faith of Jesus Christ might be given to them that believe.

23 But before faith came, we were kept under the law, shut up unto the faith which should afterwards be revealed.

24 Wherefore the law was our schoolmaster to bring us unto Christ, that we might be justified by faith.

25 But after that faith is come, we are no longer under a schoolmaster.

26 For you are all the children of God by faith in Christ Jesus.

27 For as many of you as have been baptized into Christ have put on Christ.

28There is neither Jew nor Greek, there is neither bond nor free, there is neither male nor female: for ye are all one in Christ Jesus.

29 And if you be Christ's, then are you Abraham's seed, and heirs according to the promise." (Israelite not by physical lineage, but by "adoption" into God's family) (Galatians 3:16-29)

Being in God's family is not about physical lineage, but about having His Spirit in us as His children of promise!

22 "For it is written, that Abraham had two sons, the one by a bondmaid, the other by a free-woman.

23 But he who was of the bondwoman was born after the flesh; but he of the free-woman was by promise.

²⁴ Which things are an allegory: for these are the two covenants; the one from the mount Sinai, which genders to bondage, which is Hagar.

²⁵ For this Hagar is mount Sinai in Arabia, and answers to Jerusalem which now is, and is in bondage with her children.

²⁶ But Jerusalem which is above is free, which is the mother of us all.

²⁷ For it is written, Rejoice, thou barren that bears not; break forth and cry, you that travail not: for the desolate hath many more children than she which has a husband.

²⁸ Now we, brethren, as Isaac was, are the children of promise.

²⁹ But as then he that was born after the flesh persecuted him that was born after the Spirit, even so it is now.

³⁰ Nevertheless what says the scripture? Cast out the bondwoman and her son: for the son of the bondwoman shall not be heir with the son of the free-woman.

³¹ So then, brethren, we are not children of the bondwoman, but of the free." (Galatians 4:22-31)

What is the point?

Only True Believers are ABRAHAM'S TRUE CHILDREN. As Jesus told the Pharisees, *"God is able to raise up children to Abraham from these stones."* Believers are born by God's Spirit - the miracle of the New Birth! Having the physical relation to Abraham does NOT make someone a member of God's family. So, when we read about Israel, or Israelites, or Jews, etc., unless it is specifically in a historical context or speaking of specific individuals, the passage is likely referring to TRUE BELIEVERS.

RESURRECTION RAPTURE (JOY)

*"The dead in Christ will **rise** first and we who are alive and remain will be caught up together with them, and thus we will always be with the Lord."* (1st Thessalonians 4:16)

"But now is Christ risen from the dead, and become the first-fruits of them that slept. For since by man came death, by man came also the resurrection of the dead. For as in Adam all die, even so in Christ shall all be made alive. But every man in his own order. Christ the first-fruits; afterward they that are Christ's at his coming." (1st

Corinthians 15:21-22)

"Now this I say, brethren, that flesh and blood cannot inherit the kingdom of God; neither doth corruption inherit incorruption. Behold, I shew you a mystery; We shall not all sleep, but we shall all be changed, In a moment, in the twinkling of an eye, at the last trump: for the trumpet shall sound, and the dead shall be raised incorruptible, and we shall be changed. For this corruptible must put on incorruption, and this mortal must put on immortality. So when this corruptible shall have put on incorruption, and this mortal shall have put on immortality, then shall be brought to pass the saying that is written, Death is swallowed up in victory. O death, where is thy sting? O grave, where is thy victory?" (1st Corinthians 15)

*"For all creation is waiting eagerly for that future day when **God will reveal who his children really are.** Against its will, all creation was subjected to God's curse. But with eager hope, the creation looks forward to the day when it will join God's children in glorious freedom from death and decay. For we know that all creation has been groaning as in the pains of childbirth right up to the present time. And we believers also groan, even though we have the Holy Spirit within us as a foretaste of future glory, for we long for our bodies to be released from sin and suffering. We, too, wait with eager hope for the day when God will give us our full rights as his adopted children, including the new bodies he has promised us."* (Romans 8:19-23)

GREAT RESOURCES

- FreedomForce.LIVE for links

    Sealed Indictments (170,000+)

    CEO Resignations (12,350+)

    Seized Assets (1,300 + pages)

    Executive Orders re: Human Trafficking, Corruption, and Expansion of Guantanamo Bay Federal Prison, etc.

- Stellarium.org Free Online Planetarium

- Book on the Lost Tribes of Israel - "Missing Links Discovered In Assyrian Tablets" by E. Raymond Capt

Disclaimer: The opinions expressed in this book are the author's own, and any views expressed pertaining to any individual are alleged to be facts, based upon research, until proven in a court of law.

Made in the USA
Monee, IL
08 October 2023

44171118R00144